THIS JOURNAL BELONGS TO

_____

WHEN WOMEN
WERE BIRDS

WHEN WOMEN WERE BIRDS

FIFTY-FOUR

VARIATIONS ON VOICE

TERRY TEMPEST WILLIAMS

PICADOR

A SARAH CRICHTON BOOK

FARRAR, STRAUS AND GIROUX

NEW YORK

www.picadorusa.com
www.twitter.com/picadorusa • www.facebook.com/picadorusa
picadorbookroom.tumblr.com

Picador® is a U.S. registered trademark and is used by Farrar, Straus and Giroux under license from Pan Books Limited.

For information on Picador Reading Group Guides, please contact Picador. E-mail: readinggroupguides@picadorusa.com

Grateful acknowledgment is made for permission to reprint excerpts from the following previously published material: "The Judgment of the Birds" by Loren Eiseley, from *The Immense Journey,* reprinted by permission of Random House, Inc.; *Why Birds Sing* by David Rothenberg (Basic Books, 2005), reprinted by permission of the author.

Designed by Abby Kagan
Bird art by Adly Elewa
Endpaper art by Mary Toscano

The Library of Congress has cataloged the Farrar, Straus and Giroux edition as follows:

Williams, Terry Tempest.
    When women were birds : fifty-four variations on voice / Terry Tempest Williams.—1st ed.
        p.   cm.
    ISBN 978-0-374-28897-6
    1. Williams, Terry Tempest.   2. Naturalists—United States—Biography.   3. Women naturalists—United States—Biography.   4. Mothers and daughters—Biography.   5. Mothers and daughters—Psychology.   I. Title.
    QH31.W626 W55 2012
    508.092'2—dc23   2011047161

Picador ISBN 978-1-250-02411-4

First published in the United States by Sarah Crichton Books, an imprint of Farrar, Straus and Giroux

First Picador Edition: March 2013

20 19 18 17 16 15

ANN MUDGE BACKER
Muse

•

LAURA SIMMS
Story

•

LINDA ASHER
Translator

•

ALEXANDRA FULLER
Voice

•

ALL THOSE WITH WINGS

What if there were a hidden pleasure
in calling one thing
by another's name?

—RAE ARMANTROUT

Birds, birds . . . Behold them armed for action,
like daughters of the spirit . . .
    On the white page with infinite margins,
the space they measure is all incantation.

—ST.-JOHN PERSE

GRATITUDES

A book is created in community. I would like to acknowledge Ann Mudge Backer of Surry, Maine; Annette and Ian Cumming of Jackson, Wyoming; Beatrice Monti della Corte and the Santa Maddalena Foundation in Donnini, Italy, for writing sanctuary. Mariah Hughs, Nick Sichterman: Blessings; Bonnie McDougall, Cathy Silber: Nushu; Hélène Cixous: Language; Leo Treitler: Opera; Kim Ridley, Tom Curry: Painted Bunting; Julia Barello: Swallows; Vicky and Robert Newman: Spiral Jetty; Tom Miller, Jennifer Majersik, Stan Resor, Starie Seay: Health; Laurie Graham: Faith; Mary Toscano: Feathers; Daniel Piepenbring, Abby Kagan, Rodrigo Corral, Jeff Seroy, Kathy Daneman: Farrar, Straus & Giroux; David Rogers, Elizabeth Bruce, Gabrielle Gantz: Picador; Matthew Rothschild, Ben George: Revision; Rick Bass, Lyn Dalebout, K'Lea Andreas, Mary Frank, Stephen Trimble, Monette Clark, Mickey Houlihan, Andy Friedland, Carol Folt, Laura Kamala, Eleanor Bliss, Bill Hedden, Teresa Cavazos Cohn, Bill Resor, Story Clark, Avery and Felicia Resor, Lee and Ed Riddell, Betsy Burton, Karen Shepherd, Geralyn White Dreyfous, Anne Milliken, Annabelle Milliken, Carol Stockham, Hank Tempest, Dan Tempest, Lynne Tempest, Becky Williams, Rex Williams, Steven Barclay, and Carl Brandt. Appreciation. And of course, Sarah Crichton: Vision; John Tempest, Louis Gakumba, and Brooke Williams: Home.

WHEN WOMEN
WERE BIRDS

I

I AM FIFTY-FOUR YEARS OLD, the age my mother was when she died. This is what I remember: We were lying on her bed with a mohair blanket covering us. I was rubbing her back, feeling each vertebra with my fingers as a rung on a ladder. It was January, and the ruthless clamp of cold bore down on us outside. Yet inside, Mother's tenderness and clarity of mind carried its own warmth. She was dying in the same way she was living, consciously.

"I am leaving you all my journals," she said, facing the shuttered window as I continued rubbing her back. "But you must promise me that you will not look at them until after I am gone."

I gave her my word. And then she told me where they were. I didn't know my mother kept journals.

A week later she died. That night, there was a full moon encircled by ice crystals.

On the next full moon I found myself alone in the family home. I kept expecting Mother to appear. Her absence became her presence. It was the right time to read her journals. They were exactly where she said they would be: three shelves of beautiful clothbound books; some floral, some paisley, others in solid colors. The spines of each were perfectly aligned against the lip of the shelves. I opened the first journal. It was empty. I opened the second journal. It was empty. I opened the third. It, too, was empty, as was the fourth, the fifth, the sixth—shelf after shelf after shelf, all my mother's journals were blank.

II

I DO NOT KNOW WHY my mother bought journal after journal, year after year, and never wrote in one of them and passed them on to me.

I will never know.

The blow of her blank journals became a second death.

My Mother's Journals are paper tombstones.

I am fifty-four years old, the age my mother was when she died. The questions I hold now could not have been comprehended when I was a woman in my twenties. I didn't realize how young she was, but isn't that the conceit of mothers—that we conceal our youth and exist only for our children? It is the province of mothers to preserve the myth that we are unburdened with our own problems. Placed in a circle of immunity, we carry only the crises of those we love. We mask our needs as the needs of others. If ever there was a story without a shadow, it would be this: that we as women exist in direct sunlight only.

When women were birds, we knew otherwise.

We knew our greatest freedom was in taking flight at night, when we could steal the heavenly darkness for ourselves, navigating through the intelligence of stars and the constellations of our own making in the delight and terror of our uncertainty.

What my mother wanted to do and what she was able to do remains her secret.

We all have our secrets. I hold mine. To withhold words is power. But to share our words with others, openly and honestly, is also power.

I was aware of the silences within my mother. They were her places of strength, inviolable. Tillie Olsen studied such silence. She writes,

> Literary history and the present are dark with silences . . . I have had special need to learn all I could of this over the years, myself so nearly remaining mute and having to let writing die over and over again in me. These are not natural silences—what Keats called *agonie ennuyeuse* (the tedious agony)—that necessary time for renewal, lying fallow, gestation, in the natural cycle of creation. The silences I speak of here are unnatural: the unnatural thwarting of what struggles to come into being, but cannot.

We hold these silences as a personal crucifix.

What is voice?

I will say it is so: The first voice I heard belonged to my mother. It was her voice I listened to from the womb; from the moment my head emerged into this world; from the moment I was pushed out, then placed on her belly before the umbilicus was cut; from the moment when she cradled me in her arms. My mother spoke to me: "Hello, little one. You are here, I am here."

I will say it is so: My mother's voice is a lullaby in my cells. When I am still, my body feels her breathing.

III

LIMINAL. A threshold. My body between worlds. This word returns me to my original state. *"I am water. I am water."* I am sea cells evolving to a consciousness that has pulled me upright. Walking the wrack line on a sandy beach, I pick up shells, a whelk, a cowrie, a conch, each a witness to a world we cannot see until we touch it, hold it, bring it to our ear and listen. The invisible world can speak to us. In this vast, undulating ocean, we are cradled. The waves carry us like the rise and fall of the melody of mothers. So much of who we are originates and remains here in salt water. I pick up another shell and listen . . .

My mother left me her journals, and all her journals were blank.

In Mormon culture, women are expected to do two things: keep a journal and bear children. Both gestures are a participatory bow to the past and the future. In telling a story, personal knowledge and continuity are maintained. My mother kept her journals and bore four children: a daughter and three sons. I am her daughter, in love with words. The repetitions of her journals reach me in waves. Diving beneath them is my only protection.

IV

A MOTHER and daughter are an edge. Edges are ecotones, transitional zones, places of danger or opportunity. House-dwelling tension. When I stand on the edge of the land and sea, I feel this tension, this fluid line of transition. High tide. Low tide.

It is the sea's reach and retreat that reminds me we have been human for only a very short time.

I was born on the edge of the Pacific. California was paradise. My mother took me to the beach daily near Capistrano, home to the returning swallows. While my father was in the air force, my mother and I played in the sand. It is here I must have imprinted on the rhythmic sound of waves, the cry of gulls, the calm of my own mother's heart.

It is here, on this edge of sand and surf, where I must have developed my need to see the horizon, to look outward as far and wide as possible. My hunger for vistas has never left me. And it is here I must have fallen in love with water, recognizing its power and sublimity, where I learned to trust that what I love can kill me, knock me down, and threaten to drown me with its unexpected wave. If so, then it was also here where I came to know I can survive what hurts. I believed in my capacity to stand back up and run into the waves again and again, no matter the risk. A wave would break, rush toward me, covering my feet, and retreat into the sea, followed by another and another. This was the great seduction. There was no end to the joyful exaltation on this edge of oscillations.

And each night the smell of orange blossoms and sea salt ignited sunsets into flames slowly doused by the sea. Not a year of my life has missed a baptism by ocean. Not one.

Why this relationship to Mother and water?

Breaking waters. We are born from what is fluid, not fixed. Water is essential. A mother is essential. The ocean as mother is mesmerizing in her power, a creative force that can both comfort and destroy. My mother and I came to trust each other on the beach where we sat. Between the silences, we played together. We entertained ourselves. On the edge of the continent, looking west, we came to an understanding of the peace and violence around us. Power is the sea's thundering voice, the curling and crashing of waves. Water is nothing if not ingemination, an encore to the tenacity of life. And life held in the sea is surface and depth, what we see and what we imagine. We cast a line, we throw out a net, what emerges is religion in the form of fish.

My mother's transgression was hunger. She passed her hunger on to me without ever speaking a word. Solitude is a memory of water. I live in the desert. And every day I am thirsty.

When I opened my mother's journals and read emptiness, it translated to longing, that same hunger and thirst Mother translated to me. I will rewrite this story, create my own story on the pages of my mother's journals.

V

I AM writing on the blank page of my mother's journal, not with a pen, but a pencil. I like the idea of erasure. The permanence of ink is an illusion. Ink fades and is absorbed into the paper. Water can smear it. Ink runs out. A pencil can be sharpened repeatedly and then disappear in the process. Like me. In the past, my words have been born out of flames. Today my words emerge from water. A woman's water breaks, and she goes into labor. Birth is imminent. A writer's imagination breaks loose and she, too, goes into labor.

Everything feels new. A new year. A new decade. A new blank page. I am writing on a blank page of my mother's journals, not with a pen, but a pencil. I like the idea of erasure.

ERASURE

1. to rub or scrape out, as letters or characters written, engraved, etc.; efface.
2. to eliminate completely: *She couldn't erase the tragic scene from her memory.*
3. to obliterate (material recorded on magnetic tape or a magnetic disk): *She erased the message.*

4. to obliterate recorded material from (a magnetic tape or disk): *He accidentally erased the tape.*
5. *Slang.* to murder: *She had to be erased so she would not tell the truth.*
6. to give way to effacement readily or easily.
7. to obliterate characters, letters, markings, etc., from something.
8. remove; rub out.

Origin: 1595–1605; < L *ērāsus* (ptp. of *ērādere*), equiv. to ē-<u>e-</u> + *rāsus* scraped; see <u>raze</u>

Part of Speech: verb

Synonyms:
abolish
annul
black out
blank
blot
blue-pencil
cross out
cut
cut out
delete
disannul
dispatch
efface

eliminate
excise
expunge
extirpate
gut
kill
launder
negate
nullify
obliterate
scratch out
stamp out
strike
strike out
take out
trim
wipe out
withdraw
x

Erasure. What every woman knows but rarely discusses. I don't mind erasure if it is done by my own hand. My choice. Write a word. Not the right word. Turn the pencil upside down, erase. Back and forth on the page. Pencil upright. Begin again. Point on the page. Pause. Find the right word. Write the word. Word by word, the language of women so often begins with a whisper.

I am leaving you all my journals . . .

When silence is a choice, it is an unnerving presence. When silence is imposed, it is censorship.

My Mother's Journals are an obsession.

My Mother's Journals are an obsession shared.

My Mother's Journals are a possession.

My Mother's Journals now possess me.

My Mother's Journals are desire.

My Mother's Journals are my desire to know.

My Mother's Journals are evidence.

My Mother's Journals are evidence she knew me.

My Mother's Journals are the power of absence.

My Mother's Journals are the power of presence.

VI

WHEN MY FATHER WAS OUT OF TOWN, running pipe and putting in gas lines for weeks, months, in Helper, Utah, or Baggs, Wyoming, my mother was at her most calm. For us, it constituted a holiday. Dinners were relaxed, and the household had an air of vacation, free from his intensity.

Our father was our action figure: playing catch, hiking mountains, and hunting deer. If there was a robbery in the neighborhood, he formed a posse to solve it. If there was a river to run, he ran it, be it the Green River or the Colorado or the Snake. Those waterways coursed off maps and into our veins, tattooing our father's love of wilderness into our love for him. If there was a mountain to hike or a trail to walk, I was right behind him as his daughter. The Tetons, the Wasatch, the Rocky Mountains were our collective backbone as a family.

At home each night, we ended the day with adventure stories. Our favorite was "Scarface: The Story of a Grizzly" by Dorr G. Yeager. Sitting on his knees, listening to the beautiful language about grizzlies moving among the timber, what they saw, how they smelled, the power behind one swat of their paw, we were caught not only in the emotional drama of the story but also in our father's passion in conveying such a magnificent beast. My brothers and I were rapt. First and foremost, John Tempest is a storyteller. But we always knew the clarity of one fact: he was most fulfilled when he was outside with his boots on, walking the trench line, bidding jobs of high-pressure gas lines cutting across the American West.

Mother held her own intensity, but it was contained, especially when we were alone with her. It was during these days on Moor Mont Drive in Salt Lake City that Mother introduced my brother Steve and me to Prokofiev's *Peter and the Wolf*. Whole afternoons were absorbed sitting cross-legged on the floor before our phonograph, listening to this musical tale. The minute the record ended, we would lift the needle back to the beginning and listen all over again.

I have no idea what Mother did during those hours when we were under the spell of Prokofiev, but I'm sure that was the point. Our time with Peter was her time with herself.

Through the authority of Richard Hale's British narration, Steve and I were introduced to the distinctive voices of each character: the bird was the flute; the duck was the oboe; the cat, the clarinet; the grandfather, the bassoon; and the wolf was recognized by three French horns. Peter's presence became the melody played by the strings of the orchestra. Rifle shots were rendered by the kettledrum.

"Early one morning, Peter opened the gate and went into the big green meadow. On a branch of a big tree sat a little bird, Peter's friend. 'All is quiet,' chirped the bird gaily . . ."

And the orchestral adventure began.

What I realize now is this: within those thirty minutes that took Prokofiev only four days to compose, I received my first tutorial on voice. Each of us has one. Each voice is distinct and has something to say. Each voice deserves to be heard. But it requires the act of listening.

Peter and the Wolf was also an early lesson on how the balance of nature could be articulated through story. Niche was the specificity of voice.

"Seeing the duck, the little bird flew down upon the grass, settled next to her, and shrugged his shoulders. 'What kind of a bird are you, if you can't fly?' said he. To this the duck replied, 'What kind of a bird are you if you can't swim?' And dived in the pond."

For my brother and me, the cycle of nature consciously or unconsciously was performed through the various voices of a symphony. "And if one would listen very carefully, he could hear the duck quacking inside the wolf; because the wolf in his hurry had swallowed her alive."

Listening over and over to the voices through a

family of instruments allowed us to recognize and appreciate the dignity and uniqueness of each living thing in the meadow and forest.

Peter showed us what Mother wanted us to know but didn't have to say. She may have been pretending to close the door and disappear, but she knew the lessons: Here is the world. It is not a safe place, but however frightening and bewildering life may become, we can survive our fears, grab them by the wolf's tail as Peter did, and make peace with the world.

Each voice belongs to a place. Solitude is a place. Mother left us alone to enjoy our own company while she enjoyed hers and reclaimed precious time for herself. When she wasn't living her solitude, she was contemplating it.

VII

IF MY MOTHER KEPT BLANK JOURNALS, my grandmother's journals were her field guides. Roger Tory Peterson's field guides, to be exact. Each of the field guides was bound in turquoise-green cloth. They cataloged, identified, and illustrated stars, rocks, minerals, trees, shrubs, wildflowers, shells, insects, fish, amphibians and reptiles, mammals, and birds. Her favorite guide was *A Field Guide to Western Birds*, published in 1961 by the Houghton Mifflin Company. It had a royal blue dust jacket with white print. In the upper right-hand corner a portrait of a puffin appeared, and below the title, painted inside a white rectangle, was a western tanager and an evening grosbeak.

I have my grandmother's copy on my desk. The dust jacket is worn. When I open the book, the endpapers are silhouettes of birds perched on telephone wires, a tree, and on fence posts, birds you might see driving along roadsides: a robin, a magpie, a mourning dove, a crow.

In my grandmother's script, written with her characteristic red pen, she has signed her name inside on the diagonal: "Kathryn Blackett Tempest, 1599 Orchard Drive, Salt Lake City, Utah 84106." It is written with great flourish.

On each illustrated plate, next to a particular bird, she has written the date and place where she first saw this species. For example, next to the image of a hermit thrush, she has written "1962, Bullen's Ranch."

If I cross-reference my field guide with hers, many of the species I first saw coincide with Mimi's and a memory ensues. I first saw a western tanager at my friend Gayle Platt's house. Her backyard encompassed Mill Creek, which flows through Salt Lake. In the middle of her birthday party the tanager appeared. I immediately left whatever game we were playing and followed the bird as if in a trance. This was the bird I had longed to see. Sure enough, the characteristic red head, yellow body, and black wings came into view. When Mrs. Platt followed me and asked me what I was staring at, I quickly pointed to the bird in the cottonwood tree. Irritated that I had strayed from the party, she asked me to return to the other children. I asked her if I could call my grandmother, which I did. Within minutes, Mimi drove over in her gold-finned Cadillac, and she let each girl at the party see the red, yellow, and black bird through the lens of her binoculars.

This moment is recounted in both our field guides. She gave me mine when I was five years old. It is the first book I remember taking to bed. Beneath my covers, I held a flashlight in one hand and the field guide in the other. I studied each painted bird carefully and took them into my dreams.

In a family that hunted, I learned the names of the ducks my father would shoot.

I asked him for their wings. Right wing. Left wing. And I gathered their feathers in a bouquet. When we sat down at the dinner table to eat duck, I said silent prayers for cinnamon teals and canvasbacks.

VIII

The air of the early August morn tingled with a crisp freshness. Thrushes joined with warblers in producing a medley of notes which rang throughout the woods like a great symphony orchestra. Blades of grass bent forward and back in rhythmic motions with the warm morning breeze.

My words from a journal kept in the summer of 1970. I was fourteen years old.

Mimi and I stepped out of the cabin ready to experience and observe the secrets and thrills that can be found in the world of nature. We walked with binoculars in hand so we could view the slightest detail . . . We could feel the warm sun filtering through the leaves of the aspens.

We seated ourselves on an old knotted log that had been struck with lightning many years ago and listened, listened to the silence. I heard nothing but a beautiful stillness.

My grandmother and I were staying at a family cabin in Utah's Uinta Mountains, the only mountain range in the United States to run east and west. Our destination was Bud Lake. Mimi rose early. "This is the time to see birds," she said. I trusted her, and we were in the field before dawn. As we sat on that log in emerging light, birdsong enveloped us.

The call of the birds seemed catching, for now the meadow was a place wild with excitement. Suddenly, the voice of a scrub jay could be heard violently screeching so loud as if it was a warning to all living creatures. Then, a deathly silence . . . from the ridge above flew an eagle.

We witnessed the golden eagle swoop down and grab a mouse in its talons.

Once at Bud Lake, I looked at my grandmother's face, and I felt a deep message was inside her. She was staring out at the lake and I guessed she was thinking of the soothing repeat of nature. The assurance that bare branches will bring the buds of spring, that yellow dandelions will become white with seeds, and that each life is precious unto itself . . . Mimi turned to me and said, "We are part of nature—"

Simple words, effusive words, written in the ecstatic state of youth. I found peace in an aspen grove shared with my grandmother. In this place of rich black soil sheltered by the shimmering round leaves of white-barked trees, my voice set down roots.

These handwritten words in the pages of my journal confirm that from an early age I have experienced each encounter in my life twice: once in the world, and once again on the page.

When I returned home, I read these pages to my father.

"A bit flowery," he said.

IX

A SPEECH impediment is an excellent way to lose your voice, especially in fourth grade. When most children were out playing at recess, I was sitting with Mrs. Parkinson in speech therapy. "Tongue-swallowing lessons," she said. "It has been recommended by your teacher to help you get over your lisp."

My teacher had told her I had a lisp. My face turned red, and I was flushed with embarrassment. I wasn't aware that I spoke with a lisp until I was told. We usually don't have an ear toward our own voice. Friends would make fun of me, the way kids do. Sometimes I laughed with them. Sometimes I did not. But the sure remedy to criticism and ridicule was a simple one: keep quiet.

My great fear in school was that I would be asked to read out loud. And if I was, I prayed I would be given paragraphs without the letter *s*. The old tongue twister "Sally sat by the seashore . . ." was my agony. I would try to steer the conversation toward "Peter Piper picked a peck of pickled peppers." I knew that diversion by heart.

Three times a week Mrs. Parkinson and I would meet in her special classroom full of plants and posters with illustrations of various consonant and vowel sounds. She would help me redirect my tongue when I spoke and swallowed. The point was to stop the practice of tongue thrusting.

The exercises went something like this: She would give me a saltine cracker to chew, with the instructions that I was to form a little ball in the center of my tongue. Once that feat was accomplished, I would open my mouth to show her.

Then, after much encouragement, she would place a tiny elastic band around the tip of my tongue (at least this is how I remember it) and show me with her own tongue where to place it on "the spot" (behind the ridge on the roof of my mouth).

I would position my tongue perfectly, just as she demonstrated, and then she would say, "Now swallow."

I swallowed. She watched.

"Very good."

I would go through a column of crackers each session, or so it seemed. That was the swallowing lesson. The lesson to get rid of my lisp was something different.

If I placed the tip of my tongue where I normally did when I spoke—behind my front tooth and "its neighbor" to the right—and said "Sally," I created a leaky sound like "Thally." But if I placed the tip of my tongue on the opposite side of my mouth, behind and between my left front tooth and the one next to it, I created a crisp, clean sound that was correct. "Sally." No lisp.

What was required of me was practice. Mrs. Parkinson and I read poetry together, my voice overlaying hers. She taught me how to hear the sounds of words and find delight in the rhythm and musicality of certain combinations, like the Emily Dickinson poem that begins:

Some keep the Sabbath going to church;
I keep it staying at home,
With a bobolink for a chorister,
And an orchard for a dome.

There were plenty of s words in the poem, but I didn't mind, because I so loved what the poem was saying. I forgot myself and concentrated on what was being said instead of how I said it.

One of my favorite poems we shared was called "Questioning Faces" by Robert Frost:

The winter owl banked just in time to pass
And save herself from breaking window glass.
And her wings straining suddenly aspread
Caught color from the last of evening red
In a display of underdown and quill
To glassed-in children at the window sill.

She knew I loved birds; had I told her I loved owls? It only solidified how much I admired my speech therapist, looked forward to our time together.

For homework I read these poems aloud with my mother. *"E-nun-ci-ate,"* I remember her saying slowly. The practice of speaking words clearly. Elocution. Suddenly I began to enjoy the art of speaking because it followed the art of listening. These poems were puzzles and secrets, each with its own hidden meaning. It mattered how they were spoken. My task was to honor the power of each word by delivering it as beautifully as I could.

In fourth grade I was not aware of alliteration or iambic pentameter or the symbolism of the owl as wisdom and the innocence of children in danger of colliding with fate. Nor could I have known how these themes of nature and culture would grow inside me and possess me later as a writer. I only knew the pleasure the poems were bringing to my mouth and ears. I could never explain to my friends how much I enjoyed my speech class, even if it meant missing recess. Poetry became play, a verbal athleticism more fun and challenging than playing four square or jumping hurdles on the soccer field.

Mrs. Parkinson believed in the beauty of the human voice and called my voice "an instrument." She taught me to speak with a confidence and joy I had not known before. She helped me correct the source of my embarrassment by being conscious of sounds. She insisted on listening. I no longer feared being called on to read in class, because Mrs. Parkinson introduced me to the potential of my own voice supported by skill and substance over insecurity and doubt. I emerged as a lover of words.

I did not find my voice—my voice found me through the compassion of a teacher who understood how poetry transforms us through the elegance and lyricism of language. By sharing her own love of poetry, Mrs. Parkinson inspired me to speak beyond my fearful self.

I don't believe our fears ever leave us completely. I still tremble each time I stand up to speak. I feel faint, nerves ricocheting between the confines of my own skin as memories of a childhood lisp awaken in every muscle of my body. And in those first few minutes before a group of people, my instincts shout, *Bolt now, there is still time to escape*. But then I pause, look around the room, find whose eyes are present, and orient myself like a compass, remembering that words are much stronger than I am. I take a deep breath and sidestep my fear and begin speaking from the place where beauty and bravery meet—within the chambers of a quivering heart.

X

MATILDA THOMAS was born one year ago on New Year's Day. Her father is my nephew, Nate. Her mother's name is Jinna, and she is a first-generation Korean American. In Korean tradition, on a child's first birthday she is presented with vocational objects placed on a table, representing the work of the parents, aunts and uncles, and guests. A dollar bill for wealth is included alongside a bullet or a replica of a gun to represent military service. The child stands before the objects and is invited to pick what delights her. Whatever the child chooses, tradition says this is what she will become. Pick two more, and they portend the accompanying passions. Matilda picked a cook's large spoon. *A chef.* She picked her father's BlackBerry. *A lawyer.* And her auntie's pencil. *A writer.*

I whispered in Matilda's ear when no one was looking, "A pencil is a wand and a weapon. Be careful. Protect yourself. It can be glorious."

My mother left me her journals, and all her journals were blank. Emily Dickinson wrote poems in her bedroom and kept them largely secret. The poet Susan Howe writes, "She may have chosen to enter the space of silence, a space where power is no longer an issue, gender is no longer an issue, voice is no longer an issue, where the idea of a printed book appears as a trap."

I wonder if I should have given Matilda a blank piece of paper instead.

My dear Matilda, I write you this letter with the tip of a feather dipped in blood . . .

No, that would not be fair.

My dear Matilda, I write you this letter with the tip of a feather dipped in invisible ink . . .

It was Mother who showed us how to write secret messages with lemon juice. She would pick a lemon, roll it on the counter with her hands, then slice it in half and squeeze the juice into a bowl. With paintbrushes in hand, we would write our words on parchment paper. A match was lit, the flame burned beneath the paper, what was hidden magically appeared.

My Mother's Journals are written with invisible ink.

XI

I was fascinated by what I couldn't see but would die without. *All About Air* was the book I repeatedly checked out of the library. Four gases create air: nitrogen (78.09 percent), oxygen (20.95 percent), argon (0.93 percent), and carbon dioxide (0.039 percent). Water vapor (2 percent) is also found in the atmosphere. This gave me confidence. The unseen world was real.

I would lie in a sun puddle on our living-room floor, staring at dust particles dancing in the column of light streaming above me. Using my field guide to air, I tried to differentiate flakes of dried skin from specks of dirt, sand, or salt from the sea. Smoke and pollen were in this mix, and I imagined dust mites eating the microscopic flecks floating in the air, swirling around us all the time, too tiny to see. The sun became an honest broker in showing me what we breathe. But what thrilled me most was the fact that millions of meteors burn up every day as they enter our atmosphere. As a result, Earth receives ten tons of dust from outer space. Not only do we take in the world with each breath, we are inhaling the universe. We are made of stardust.

*My Mother's Journals are part nitrogen, part
oxygen, part argon, part carbon dioxide, and
water vapor, with all its invisible particles.*

"The stars are our ancestors," write Mary Evelyn
Tucker and Brian Swimme in *The Journey of the Universe*. "Out of them, everything comes forth . . . For
stars, creativity depends on maintaining a state of
disequilibrium . . . It is the dynamic tension between
gravity and fusion . . . outward expansion and contraction . . . Stars are wombs of immense creativity."

*My Mother's Journals are an expanding and
collapsing universe each time they are opened
and closed.*

XII

IN THE ARID FOOTHILLS of the Wasatch Mountains, the Milky Way arched over us. It was the
nightly path our eyes crossed before we went to sleep.
This was my personal universe, with its own inherent
truths. Truth, for me, was based on what I could see
and hear, touch and taste, more trustworthy than any

religious doctrine. Indoor religion bored me; outdoor religion did not. Rufous-sided towhees scratched in the understory of last year's leaves; lazuli buntings were turquoise exclamation marks singing in a canopy of green; and blue-gray gnatcatchers became commas in an ongoing narrative of wild nature. My inspiration was winged. Magpies, evening grosbeaks, and scrub jays were family. Turkey vultures soared overhead, casting unexpected shadows during summer heat. Rattlesnakes were our complication to a life lived outside. We heard them first; saw them second, coiled; and before we counted to three, we ran. Clouds became our focal point for change.

The minute school ended, our game of "Capture" began. It was our form of *Treasure Island* in the mountains. Children in the neighborhood begin building and rebuilding last year's tree houses in the scrub oak.

I cannot tell you what the point of this ongoing game was, only that it consumed us from the moment we awoke until dinnertime. We spied on one another, girls against boys, from the vantage point of trees. The sweet pleasure of imagining I was someone else living somewhere else was enough to capture me for an entire summer.

We made up our own language. We drew maps. We buried them. We created a community with our own currency from found pieces of glass. Green and brown shards were common. Lavender was sought after, blue glass was rare, but red was the gleam you looked for beneath the hot desert sun shining through the understory of sage.

One day, however, as I was sitting in our tree house, I spotted a white bird perched directly above me. It was unlike anything I had ever seen. I went into the house to call my grandmother, still watching the ghost bird through the glass sliding doors that faced the trees. I explained the size and shape of this mysterious bird to be that of a robin, only without a brown back, black head, and red breast. She listened carefully. We both had our bird books in hand. "Perhaps it is an albino," she said. "A bird without pigmentation, even its eyes without color." That very word, *albino*, was a revelation to me. She might as well have said *of the spirit world*.

It was indeed a robin, the most common of birds, free of its prescribed dressings, white with red eyes. I was inspired and called her "the Holy Ghost."

When I reported this finding to our local Audubon chapter as an eight-year-old bird-watcher, the president said that because of my age, he could not legitimately count it as "a credible sighting."

My grandmother simply shook her head and said, "You know what you saw. The bird doesn't need to be counted, and neither do you."

XIII

WHAT NEEDS TO BE COUNTED on to have a voice? Courage. Anger. Love. Something to say; someone to speak to; someone to listen. I have talked to myself for years in the privacy of my journals. The only things I've done religiously are keep a journal and use birth control. My first journal had a lock and key. It was a diary made of light blue leather embossed with a gold border. My thoughts and secrets were safe from my brothers. It was a gift from my great-grandfather Lawrence Blackett, Mimi's father, to commemorate my eighth birthday and baptism into the Mormon Church.

A diary differs from a journal in expectations. A diary asks for a daily entry. This I could not do. Almost immediately I transformed my diary into a journal, where I could write in its pages at will. I still recall one entry in particular because it was written in code:

Decisions . . .
    Decisions . . .
        Decisions . . .
We finally made it to Jackson Hole.

It conveyed a descending sense of disappointment, and then resolution. The reason I can retrieve this passage almost five decades later is because of the dilemma it posed. Do I tell the truth on the page or disguise my feelings in words that will be understood only by me? This required skillfulness. I would protect myself and those I loved, giving nothing away. I didn't want to criticize my father.

I didn't want to whine (forbidden in our family). But I needed to define my frustration. I called on style, symbols, and shorthand. I learned early how to cover myself as a writer should the lock be picked and my words read.

What I wanted to say was that in our family, work came first. We never knew one minute to the next whether we would ever go on vacation until we were actually in the car. Uncertainty was certain. Everything depended on the state of the Tempest Company, a family-run pipeline business. If Dad was needed, we stayed home. When he was free, we were on the road. Tense negotiations between our parents often surfaced beyond their bedroom. Would Mother drive us up alone? Would Dad come up later? Or would they drive up together the next day, with my brothers and me traveling earlier with our aunt and uncle and cousins?

I was frustrated. We had been waiting all day. Finally a decision was made. Yes, we would be going to the Tetons. I had a record of my complaint.

"What's in those diaries then?"

"They aren't diaries."

"Whatever they are."

"Chaos, that's the point."

—Doris Lessing,
The Golden Notebook

Mormon women write. This is what we do, we write for posterity, noting the daily happenings of our lives. Keeping a journal is keeping a record. And I have hundreds of them, hundreds of journals filled with feathers, flowers, photographs, and words. Without locks, open on my shelves. I have more journals still with field notes from the Arctic to Africa, to days spent at the Prado, to time shared among prairie dogs. Daybooks with calendars, shopping lists, and accounting figures are strewn across our home. I cannot think without a pen in hand. If I don't write it down, it doesn't exist.

Mother knew this about me. She also knew and more than understood the Mormon promptings to become a scribe. In our possession, passed down from mother to daughter, we have many journals written in the most elegant script by our forebearers, especially women who practiced polygamy. I take personal pride in a journal entry made by my great-great-grandmother, who chastises her husband for taking a third wife who was "a pretty but sickly little thing, unfit to lift a hoe in the fields or bring in a bushel of sugar beets, adding to my burden of household chores . . . one can only speculate why she was brought home in the first place."

Mother was a private woman, not a silent one. She would often say, "I don't like people knowing my thoughts." She was a Coyote, a trickster, a woman deflecting an interest in her to an interest in others. In my mother's presence, you were heard. And she always left knowing a lot more about you than you knew about her. She preferred it that way. She was warm and gracious in public, but she was a master at maintaining her privacy. Intimacy was on her terms.

When Mother did share, and she shared deeply with those closest to her, her eyes were penetrating. "What do you think?" she would ask. It makes sense that what she bequeathed to me was a mystery.

My Mother's Journals are an act of defiance.

My Mother's Journals are an act of aggression.

My Mother's Journals are an act of modesty.

To be read. To be heard. To be seen. I want to be read, I want to be heard. I don't need to be seen. To write requires an ego, a belief that what you say matters. Writing also requires an aching curiosity leading you to discover, uncover, what is gnawing at your bones. Words have a weight to them. How you choose to present them and to whom is a matter of style and choice. Yet the emptiness of my mother's journals carries the weight of a question, many questions.

My Mother's Journals are an interrogation.

XIV

MOTHER and Mimi were sitting in Mimi's living room sharing a lengthy and heated discussion about theology. I listened. Their conversation was about women holding the priesthood and having equal authority with men before God. Mimi argued that the power structure of the Mormon Church would never allow women to have parity, because central to the religion is the subjugation of women.

Mother said, "The men can have their priesthood. Who wants it? Women have their own power, and it doesn't have to be codified." Mother expressed her love for the gospel, her belief in Christ, and how she was very comfortable with her power as a woman and mother within the Church.

Mimi pushed further, calling the twelve apostles "old goats" afraid of sex, therefore obsessed with it.

She went so far as to call the Mormon Church "demonic" in its arrogance and superiority. At that time, prior to 1978, African Americans were not allowed to hold the priesthood, their dark skin evidence of past ancestral sins tied to Cain and the murder of his brother, Abel.

"How do you account for both sexism and racism?" Mimi asked. "These are the prejudices of man, not God. The Mormon god is very, very small." And then she quoted Joseph Campbell. "I believe in a God beyond God."

I felt as though I were at a tennis match watching the ball fly back and forth across the net between players with speed and agility.

"I'll bet you felt differently when you were raising your sons," Mother said.

"Yes, I did," Mimi responded, "but that was more than forty years ago. I hope I have changed from the woman I was at thirty-five to the woman I am at seventy." She looked at Mother. "The world is changing, Diane. We are living at a transitional time in history. The Church will have to change because the women in the Church are changing."

Mother stood up. "There are some truths that endure." As she walked out the door, she turned and said, "Kathryn, I don't ever want to hear another negative comment about the Church spoken in front of my children again."

Mother left. I was staying overnight. Mimi and I were on her front porch when she picked up her clippers and said matter-of-factly, "Diane is about to leave the Church." Mimi leaned into her garden and cut a bouquet of tea roses, pale yellow tinged with pink. "Let's put them in a vase, shall we, dear?"

XV

CONVERSATION is the vehicle for change. We test our ideas. We hear our own voice in concert with another. And inside those pauses of listening, we approach new territories of thought. A good argument, call it a discussion, frees us. Words fly out of our mouths like threatened birds. Once released, they may never return. If they do, they have chosen a home and the bird-words are calmed into an ars poetica. The women in my family didn't always agree, but it was in their company I felt inspired and safe.

What is birdsong but "truth in rehearsal"?

XVI

WHEN MY PERIOD CAME for the first time, I called Mother from school. I was in the eighth grade.

"It's here," I said.

"I'll be right there," she replied.

Once home, she made me a bath of rose petals.

XVII

I AM MY MOTHER, but I'm not.
I am my grandmother, but I'm not.
I am my great-grandmother, but I'm not.

Four generations of women were present in my family: my great-grandmother, Vilate Lee Romney; my grandmother, Lettie Romney Dixon; my mother, Diane Dixon Tempest; and myself.

These were the words I spoke at a meeting within the Mormon Church known as stake conference. I knew my capacity to speak was in direct relationship to the women I descended—ascended—from.

On that day, September 12, 1971, the weather system around our household was uncertainty. Mother had just been diagnosed with an aggressive form of breast cancer. It had spread to her lymph nodes. Her prognosis was not good. The doctor had told her, when pressed, that maybe, if she was lucky, she had "two years." She was thirty-eight years old, the mother of four children under fifteen. My father buried himself in work like walking into a desert sandstorm among shifting dunes, unable to see.

I watched Mother retreat. I watched Mother become steel. She was finding a different voice for herself, one that required a new vocabulary that included her needs, not ours, not only to heal, but to survive. And I watched her reading constantly, sitting in her plaid chair with her legs outstretched on the ottoman. Next to her was a Diet Coke with ice, a lime, and a straw.

She loved biographies of women: *Woman to Woman* by Gloria Vanderbilt. So moved by the author's passion for quilts, Mother had one quilt square made by a friend of hers framed, and hung it in her bathroom, where she saw it first thing in the morning. When I asked her why this mattered, she said, "It represents how women piece together their lives from the scraps left over for them."

Churchill was a hero of hers, and Mother was obsessed with his speeches. When she and her girl-friend traveled to Europe, crossing the Atlantic on the *Queen Mary* in 1952, the first item on Mother's checklist was to hear Winston Churchill speak in Parliament, which she did, twice. Mother embodied his quote "We make a living by what we get, but we make a life by what we give."

Mother respected the Mormon poet Carol Lynn Pearson, a progressive thinker writing within the framework of motherhood. *Beginnings* became a template for expanding doctrine into emancipation—these lines from "My Season":

> And all your
> Faithless doubts
> Will not destroy
> The rising spring
> In me.

And she enrolled in feminist theory classes at the University of Utah, where Annette Kolodny's classic, *The Lay of the Land: Metaphor as Experience and History in American Life and Letters*, was pored over and studied along with Susan Griffin's *Woman and Nature*. She underlined this passage: "We Enter a New Space . . . Space filled with the presence of mothers, and the place where everyone is a daughter . . . The place where she predominates . . . Her feeling of having room. The space she fills. A motion circling the void . . ."

My Mother's Journals are a motion circling the void.

And then Mother underlined "<u>We are disorderly</u>." This under the heading "What Lies Under Our Stillness."

But she was not above trash, all things Hollywood, from movie magazines like *Photoplay* and *Silver Screen* to Jacqueline Susann's 1966 bestseller, *Valley of the Dolls*, about uppers and downers and the women who rose to fame and fell. Gossip was good. She was one of the deepest women I knew and one of the most shallow. The spine of that novel became part of the scenery of our household.

As her daughter, I was trying to find my own way in the world. This was the emerging moment in American society when civil rights, women's rights, and the environmental movement were finding their voices within the context of a divisive war between generations. Vietnam for me was a POW/MIA silver bracelet worn around my wrist that bore the name Capt. Robert Willett, Jr. My soldier was never found. I would later find out Captain Willett was from Great Falls, Montana, married just six weeks before he went to war. He was a pilot whose F100 Super Saber

Jet was shot down over Laos on April 17, 1969. He is still Missing in Action, among the six hundred American soldiers lost in Laos whose fates remain unknown.

Confusion spread like water seeping through every cultural crack. The day I sluffed high school was the day I went to see *Pink Flamingos* at the University of Utah. I thought I was going to a documentary about birds. No one told me it was a film about a drag queen named Divine who relocates to Boise, Idaho.

Too stunned to leave, I watched every taboo being shattered by an ax. Blood, filth, feces, and a slab of raw meat carried between Divine's legs in a grocery store were the images before me. I returned home speechless, my eyes wide open.

Facing the death of one's mother puts things in acute perspective. I did not have the luxury of fighting with my mom as other friends did with theirs, nor did I have much tolerance for the importance of football games and the Pep Club, of which, unfortunately, I was president. I tried to resign. A rupture was occurring in me. What mattered most was time with family, time in nature, and time with myself.

Good friends were traded for good reads. Books became my moral grounding, my way of finding a philosophy that comforted me when church did not. *Siddhartha* by Hermann Hesse became sacred text. I could sit by the creek near our home and take in these words:

Blue was blue, river was river, and if also in the blue and the river, in Siddhartha, the singular and divine lived hidden, so it was still that very divinity's way and purpose, to be here yellow, here blue, there sky, there forest, and here Siddhartha. The purpose and the essential properties were not somewhere behind the things, they were in them, in everything.

At the heart of my emerging voice was the belief that nature held the secret to harmony and unity, not just outside us, but inside us, no separation. Gregor Samsa being transformed into a beetle allowed me to believe that I, too, could wake up one day transformed. Kafka's *Metamorphosis* was creative nonfiction. What appeared strange on the page, "As Gregor Samsa awoke one morning from uneasy dreams he found himself transformed in his bed into a gigantic insect," seemed not only plausible to me, but desirable. I have carried this sentence with me since 1973: "And at all costs he must not lose consciousness now, precisely now . . ."

Our parents' consciousness was never orthodox. We were homeschooled for a season in Hawaii in the height of puka shell necklaces and macramé bracelets. Puff the Magic Dragon lived exactly where we were camping in Hanalei. And hippies were a common sighting for us. There was a joke circulating among Mormons that we told with great glee: "What do you get when you mix LSD with LDS?" Answer: A high priest.

The wild, windswept beaches of the 1960s were holy, with little development.

Backpacking, Sundays were no different from Mondays. And when we hiked the Na Pali Coast as a family, as we passed one nudist commune after another in the lush, folding cliffs of Kauai above the crashing surf, my brothers and I watched our parents' envy. Responsibility was a garment they could not shed.

When I proclaimed my history and my sovereignty at the same time, standing behind the pulpit in front of my religious community, even then I knew I was breaking taboo. I couldn't have said exactly why, but I knew enough to know that we were expected to follow an unbreakable pattern through time even though our Mormon history was brief. But religious history is rooted in personal history. Especially with Joseph Smith. His hunger for truth created a vision. What is evolution if not creative adaptation and the progression of our own souls?

I was not rebelling by smoking dope or drinking, I was testing ideas. I was experimenting with voice, what I could say and still be heard in an atmosphere of prescribed truths.

When I said, "I am my mother, but I'm not," I was saying my path would be my own.

It was my grandmother Lettie who read me right. In a tender moment she told me a story about herself and my grandfather. "I don't know if I ever told you this story, darling, about the time when Sank was flying back to Boston to play tennis in the Davis Cup. I was driving him to the airport. It was early in the morning, and I was still in my nightgown. People didn't fly much in those days, and he was really rather frightened. I like to think he wanted me for companionship, not for reassurance, but at the very last minute, with his luggage in hand, standing at the gate, hesitant to board, he said, 'Lettie, come with me.' And I did. I quickly bought a little beaded Indian belt that had Utah spelled on its back, cinched it around my nightgown, and we flew away together for a very glamorous affair." She paused with a wry smile and said, "Mother never knew, nor would Father have approved. But I never forgot where I was from."

XVIII

IT IS WINTER. Ravens are standing on a pile of bones—black typeface on white paper picking an idea clean. It's what I do each time I sit down to write. What else are we to do with our obsessions? Do they feed us? Or are we simply scavenging our memories for one gleaming image to tell the truth of what is hunting us?

"To write," Marguerite Duras remarked, "is also not to speak. It is to keep silent. It is to howl noiselessly."

Today there is a fresh field of snow—no visitations by ravens, just a pristine landscape wiped clean by a blizzard. What I wouldn't give to follow my mother's tracks before she covered them up with her silence.

My mother was a great reader. She left me her journals, and all her journals were blank. I believe she wanted them read. How do I read them now?

I am afraid of silence. Silence creates a pathway to peace through pain, the pain of a distracted and frantic mind before it becomes still.

XIX

Fear seeks noisy company and pandemonium to scare away the demons.

—C. G. Jung

I fear silence because it leads me to myself, a self I may not wish to confront. It asks that I listen. And in listening, I am taken to an unknown place. Silence leaves me alone in a place of feeling. It is not necessarily a place of comfort.

The Roman goddess of silence, Angerona, held her finger to her lips as she stood in the posture of both pain and peace. My mother knew herself, and she kept her silence as a possession. It was hers alone. She didn't have to write about it.

I do.

On Friday, August 29, 1952, a pianist named David Tudor stepped onto the stage at the Maverick Concert Hall in Woodstock, New York. He sat down on the piano bench, closed the black lid over the ivory keys, and clicked a stopwatch he held in his hand. During this time he was turning the pages of a silent score. He stood twice, to open and close the piano lid between movements. After four minutes and thirty-three seconds, the pianist stood up to receive applause. The audience was stunned.

This was John Cage's masterpiece.

"What they thought was silence, because they didn't know how to listen, was full of accidental sounds." John Cage remembered that premiere performance in the Catskills, now known as *4′33″*. "You could hear the wind stirring outside during the first movement. During the second, raindrops began pattering the roof, and during the third the people themselves made all kinds of interesting sounds as they talked or walked out."

Silence introduced in a society that worships noise is like the Moon exposing the night. Behind darkness is our fear. Within silence our voice dwells. What is required from both is that we be still. We focus. We listen. We see and we hear. The unexpected emerges. John Cage sees the act of listening as the act of creation.

"It is not a question of having something to say," he would answer in a fictional dialogue between an uncompromising teacher and an unenlightened student. "Relevant action is theatrical."

4'33" was theatrical.

My Mother's Journals are theatrical.

John Cage's silent concerto was considered a scandal inspired by another scandal. One act of courage begets another, especially in art. In 1951, the American artist Robert Rauschenberg created *White Paintings*, a seven-panel exploration of white, 72 inches by 125 inches by 1 1/2 inches, oil on canvas. When it was first exhibited at the Stable Gallery in October 1953, it shocked the art world. There was no acceptable narrative that could be attached to it except, *What does this mean?*

"This particular group of works," said Rauschenberg, "were somehow sort of icons of eccentricities . . . they didn't fit into the art world at that time. I did them to see how far, you know, you could push an object and yet, it'd still mean something . . . There was a kind of courage that was built into them in their uniqueness. Most of the work in this collection scared the shit out of me, too, and they didn't stop frightening me."

During this time John Cage was deep into Zen Buddhism. He gave a talk at Vassar College, where he said, "There should be a piece that had no sounds in it. One can imagine a breathing space." In a later interview he said, "The thing that gave me the courage to do it finally . . . was seeing the white empty paintings of Bob Rauschenberg to which I responded immediately." The composer saw the *White Paintings* as "landing strips" for light and shadow. What Rauschenberg executed was something akin to silence.

Rauschenberg was not the first artist, however, to experiment with the power and palette of white. The Russian artist Kazimir Malevich painted a large, asymmetrical white square tipped inside a larger white square. He titled it *White on White*. He called this departure from painting the visible world "suprematism," defined as "the supremacy of pure feeling or perception." He painted his white squares in 1918, the year after the Russian Revolution.

"White is energy—impulse—it is question and answers—it is total in its spirit," writes Richard Pousette-Dart. "White is something you endlessly return to."

Wassily Kandinsky calls white "the harmony of silence."

If John Cage and Robert Rauschenberg are conceptual artists, then perhaps my mother is a conceptual artist as well. Are her "white" journals the contrapuntal gesture of a woman making her own private critique of cultural expectations?

Was Mother creating a parody of women's journals, the wasted time we spend writing instead of living? Why look back on the page when we can be present with the moment?

Is it a brutal rejection of solipsism, her call for engaging with the world rather than the self?

My Mother's Journals are a transgression.

My Mother's Journals are a scandal of white.

My Mother's Journals are a "harmony of silence."

I think of the desert. At high noon the desert radiates white. If any place holds silence, it is here. *Silence—that is time you are hearing.* I feel it as a vibration more than the absence of sound. Yet, as Cage suggests, "there is no such thing as an empty space or an empty time. In fact, try as we may to make silence, we cannot."

There is always something to see, something to hear. There are ambient sounds all around us, even in silence, especially in silence: wind, birdsong, insects. Perhaps the silence Cage is honoring is the stillness we seek in the natural world, born of solitude, where our capacity to listen is heightened by our ability to embrace quiet.

In the desert I often whisper. Junipers are excellent sounding boards. They have been shaped by wind. Rocks seem to care nothing about what I say, yet when I speak to them, they feel porous, capable of receiving my words and taking them in as part of their history of brokenness.

My Mother's Journals are capable of receiving my words.

I return to John Cage. During World War II he sought the softer notes. "Half-intellectually and half-sentimentally, when the war came along, I decided to use only quiet sounds. There seemed to be no truth, no good, in anything big in society. But quiet sounds were like loneliness, or love or friendship."

This feels equally true now as we find ourselves a nation at war again. We are engaged in two wars, big wars with big costs. The only thing quiet about them is that the conflicts in Afghanistan and Iraq have remained largely hidden, denied except to those who are fighting them. This is our national lie, that somehow these wars exist outside of us. America's War on Terror has silenced us, turned us into sleepwalkers, not only unable to speak, but afraid to speak out. In times of war we can use our voices as a stay against those who are suffering. In times of war, survival depends on listening to that suffering. Cage understood how the unexpected action of deep listening can create a space of transformation capable of shattering complacency and despair. He bravely called for silence as an intentional stillness that could infiltrate our imaginations: "Then we should be capable of answering the question, 'What ought we to do?'"

XX

MIMI THOUGHT she would go blind before she went deaf, so we became part of her "audio project." It began on our backs in her living room. Typically, when we were staying overnight and comfortable in our pajamas, Mimi invited us to "stretch out." My brother Steve took one chaise longue and I lay down on the other. Mimi turned off the lights, lit the candles, and told us to close our eyes. "We should learn the songs of birds," she said.

We were transported to *An Evening in Sapsucker Woods*, one of the first comprehensive recordings of birdsongs produced by the Cornell Laboratory of Ornithology in 1958. For the next hour we listened to a myriad of birds calling from these woods in upstate New York. We recognized the familiar hermit thrush, with its clear, melodious trill resounding in the cathedral of birch and pine. We knew the white-throated sparrow's call as "Peabody, Peabody, Peabody." And we became fascinated by birds unknown to us, such as the cerulean warbler or the swamp sparrow. With screams from the barred owl competing with bull-frogs, we doubted that some of the birds were birds at all.

In time, we let the names of the birds go and just sank into the reverie of sound. We fell asleep. We learn what we are supposed to learn at night.

The next morning, my brother and I awoke in the living room with blankets over us.

Mimi eventually found a hand recorder, called the "audible auditron," created by the Audubon Society. You insert a particular bird card into the hand-held device, push the button, and immediately that particular bird's song is played. We took this into the field, and various birds responded. Black-capped chickadees were always reliable. Within minutes a half dozen curious individuals would surround us with their *chick-a-dee-dee, chick-a-dee-dee-dee*s. Other birds were more wary, but if we had patience, catbirds and goldfinches answered. We made a checklist of birdsongs, not only heard but sung back to us.

My friend David Rothenberg jams with birds. He's played jazz with a white-crested laughing thrush at the National Aviary in Pittsburgh. They have improvised and made music together, created charged riffs by both listening and taking cues from each other. For David, this is not unusual. He also plays with lyre-birds in Australia and all manner of winged ones around the world.

He tells a story about another clarinetist, Henri Akoka, who was captured by the Germans in World War II and sent to a POW camp with the French composer Olivier Messiaen. Before they were taken as prisoners, Messiaen would lose himself at dawn as he listened to birdsong while sitting in the trenches, on guard for the enemy. From boyhood on, Messiaen had been transcribing the notes of birds, although he had not yet integrated them into a piece of music. Now was the time. Other musicians had been interned with them, a cellist and a violinist.

Deep inside the dark folds of prison, Messiaen went about composing one of the most soulful pieces of chamber music ever created, *Quartet for the End of Time*.

Rothenberg continues the story in his evocative book, *Why Birds Sing*:

A German officer in the camp, Karl-Albert Brüll, heard of Messiaen's prowess and made sure he was provided with music paper . . . The Red Cross provided a few musical instruments, although there were 30,000 prisoners and only a few violins and cellos and just one piano. Akoka had managed to retain his clarinet. Messiaen persevered . . . In the first movement the clarinet and violin trade sounds from blackbird and nightingale, and the solo clarinet in the third movement is a musical attempt to link the endless enthusiasm of singing birds with the long, dark weight of eternity.

"The birds," Messiaen wrote in his notes to the piece, "are the opposite of time. They represent our longing for light, for stars, for rainbows, and for jubilant song." . . . The piece was premiered in the stalag on January 15, 1941, in the midst of the most terrible war humanity has known.

We live among a gratitude of birds.

Each bird may sing differently from time to time.
Each species may sing differently from place to place.
A song may be repetitional or it may be random and
    unpredictable.
The more highly developed the song, the greater the
    range of variation.

These singer-songwriters, including larks, achieve
unique repertoires and, because the older birds'
singing influences younger ones, contribute to the
local dialect.

—John Bevis, *Aaaaw to Zzzzzd:*
The Words of Birds

The dialect I learned to recognize as a child was
the western meadowlark's song: *"Salt Lake City is a
pretty-little-place."* No other bird expressed such loy-
alty. They were the cheerleaders of our city who wore
yellow sweaters with a confident black "V" across their
chests. This lyrical phrase sung continuously in the
spring was the hometown trill that rippled through
the grasslands of the foothills where we lived.

Thanks to Mimi's fear of becoming blind, I know
most birds by sound as well as sight, certainly by heart.
Birds remain my compass points. Wherever I am, the
winged ones orient me: a red-winged blackbird in a
marsh; a willet on a beach; a kestrel hovering in a field.
In truth, birds led me to my husband.

XXI

U SUALLY I stocked new books on the shelves at Sam Weller's Bookstore, but on this particular day I was behind the counter, up front, at the cash register. A friend of mine walked into the store with a very handsome man, blond and suntanned, with unruly hair. We said hello, and the couple disappeared into the stacks.

When the two returned, the blond wild man was carrying a dozen books. I was impressed, for among his stack were some of my favorites: *Desert Solitaire* by Edward Abbey, *Black Elk Speaks*, Edward Curtis's *Portraits from North American Indian Life*, *Ceremony* by Leslie Marmon Silko, *Encounters with the Archdruid* by John McPhee, and *Wilderness and the American Mind* by Roderick Nash. He also had Peterson's *Field Guide to Western Birds*. I tried to be inconspicuous as I entered the price of each book in the register, listening carefully to their conversation.

"My dream in life is to one day own all the Peterson field guides," the man said passionately.

My friend looked at him and said, "That is the dumbest thing I have ever heard."

Without thinking, I interrupted. "I already have them—"

Our eyes met. "Brooke Williams," he said.

Surrounded by mirrors, Brooke and I were married on June 2, 1975, in the Salt Lake Temple. We knelt at either end of an altar, holding hands, as our extended family circled us. As I looked into Brooke's eyes and he looked into mine, behind us were the multiplying illusions of future worlds made in our own image, populated by our unborn children. There were no shadows, only the bright, blinding projection of the one you loved through "time and all eternity." The expectation was nothing short of becoming gods and goddesses of our own planets. Procreation was the commanding vow of marriage.

One year earlier I had been a student at the Teton Science School. Ted Major was the director, charismatic and direct. He also came from a Mormon background, having been raised in Salt Lake City. He and his brother, Jack, were expert backcountry skiers, familiar with the famed powder snow in Alta, Utah. Ted became part of the Tenth Mountain Division during World War II with David Brower and later taught biology in Alaska.

He and his wife, Joan, moved to Wyoming to work on a ranch and eventually ended up in Jackson, where Ted returned to what he loved most, teaching. He and Joan started a small summer field school in Wilson, Wyoming, in 1968, with the support of friends, including the biologist Frank Craighead, the geologist David Love, and the conservationist Mardy Murie. It was radical for its time, evolving into the first environmental education center in America. I responded to an ad in the Utah Audubon newsletter about a weekend ecology course in the Tetons led by Dr. Florence Krall, a professor of education at the University of Utah.

Driving up to Jackson Hole, Wyoming, and seeing flocks of sandhill cranes dancing in the fields outside Cokeville, Wyoming, I was certain this was a new phenomenon seen for the first time, and immediately called my ornithology professor at the University of Utah, Dr. William H. Behle, from a phone booth.

"How sweet of you to call, Terry," he said with considerable grace. "The cranes have actually been doing their mating dance for close to nine million years." He paused. "But it doesn't make it any less thrilling."

Ted Major met my hunger to know more about the natural world. He and Flo Krall created a dialogue of inquiry. The lodgepole pines I had seen as red and dying were now part of the story they introduced as fire ecology, with pine bark beetles entering the cambium layer of the tree, killing it, and preparing it for fire. Ted spoke of the flames rising with the heat in the forest, splitting open the cones that drop their seeds in the seared soil for the lodgepole's regeneration the following year.

"Lodgepole pinecones may remain unopened for years and burst open only during a forest fire," Ted said. "They are referred to as serotinous cones."

As a young Mormon woman, I heard "Resurrection."

Ted Major cared more about the questions and less about the answers.

I couldn't count all the times Ted said, "I don't know." This inspired me. I found myself participating in a language previously unknown to me, interrelated and interconnected. I didn't want to leave. My curiosity was insatiable.

Ted Major was the first Democrat I had ever met, an old-fashioned progressive who echoed César Chávez: "In a damaged human habitat, all problems merge." When we talked about natural history, we talked about politics. "We need education and laws to protect what is wild," he would say. Law, history, religion, racism, speciesism, health were all under the rubric of responsible citizenry. Ted was a true patriot. His love of country included wilderness.

It was also the first time I had been introduced to the word *ecology*. I was eighteen years old.

Before I left, Ted asked if I would take a packet of materials back to a friend of his at the university. His name was David Raskin, a professor of psychology and a leading expert in polygraphs. He had tested Patty Hearst, the publishing mogul William Hearst's daughter, who was kidnapped and joined the Symbionese Liberation Army in the 1970s.

The next day, I knocked on Dr. Raskin's door. A black-bearded, very intense man opened the door. Clearly, he didn't want to be bothered. I quickly introduced myself, told him that I had just returned from the Teton Science School and that Ted Major asked me to deliver this packet.

"How was it?" he asked.

I burst into tears.

"That bad?"

"No, that good," I said.

"Come in."

A friendly errand turned into an hour-long conversation—or perhaps, more to the point, a therapy session. No lie-detector test was needed. By the end of the hour, David Raskin sat back in his chair, his hands clasped behind his head.

"It just so happens there is a scholarship in environmental studies in our department, and it just so happens that the deadline for applying is today. And—it just so happens no one has applied."

In the next fifteen minutes I applied and was accepted, and we designed a summer project that would allow me to return to the Teton Science School. I would study tourist behavior in Grand Teton National Park.

The scholarship was for five hundred dollars. With a quick phone call from Raskin, Grand Teton National Park agreed to pay me three dollars a day, and I went back to the Science School as their first intern. I was also assigned to conduct Saturday morning bird walks as a naturalist.

In typical Tempest fashion, our entire family drove me up to the Science School, where I would be living for the summer. Ted and my father got along surprisingly well. They both liked to argue. Each thought he was right. And they both loved the mountains. My mother was charming, softening the edges of whatever tensions arose, and Joan missed nothing. Hands were shaken. Hugs were shared. And tears fell as I said goodbye to my two younger brothers, Dan and Hank. Mother gave me a framed broadside of quotes from Henry David Thoreau with a note that said "May you find your own Walden Pond."

My family left, and I walked to my cabin to unpack my Levi's, hiking boots, a few cowboy shirts, and books, one of which was *Walden*.

Toward the end of the summer I accompanied Ted and Joan on a seven-day backpacking trip into the Wind Rivers. We camped high in the Titcomb Basin, where Wyoming's highest peak came into view: Gannett Peak, elevation 13,804 feet.

Very near to its summit, we watched a coyote run up the snowfield at full bore. It stopped, turned around, sat on the snow, and looked out at the view. Any boundaries I felt as a human being toward other creatures dissolved. We, too, were partaking of the view.

When we returned home, a skinned coyote was hanging by its neck from the crossbar of the ranch as we drove into the school. Ted was driving the school bus.

He stopped, got out, cut the rope with his buck knife always on his belt, and the coyote was released into his arms. We got out of the bus and circled around him.

"This used to be the Elbo Ranch," he said. "Some of the old-timers don't like what we're doing."

I wrote Mimi a letter describing what had happened. She wrote back, "We evolve as human beings through our imagination and will. However hard it must have been for you to see this act of cruelty, view it as an insight to those who wielded the knife." I thought about the man who skinned the coyote and the man who cut it off the beam, both using the same weapon, both powerful gestures. If one can mark a moment, this was mine. I became part of the "Coyote Clan." I made a vow to the coyote who climbed Gannett Peak and the coyote who was murdered and martyred at the Elbo Ranch that I would not remain silent.

My Mother's Journals are a gesture and a vow.

I met a man named Brooke who understood wildness, and I married him. He understood when I threw back my head and howled. We were refugees held captive for too long in an orthodoxy that had become a windowless room of repression and restraint. He spoke through the physical joy of his body. He had climbed Gannett Peak when I met him, hiking the steep mountains in summers, skiing the steep and deep slopes in winters. His favorite book from childhood was *The Little Prince*. His favorite line, "Be aware of what can never be tamed."

XXII

THE PROTOCOL for teachers was severe. We were to refer to one another only by our last names and never utter our first. I was Mrs. Williams even though I was only twenty-one years old. After each class the children would make a line, and before leaving, they were obliged to shake my hand and say, "Thank you for the beautiful lesson, Mrs. Williams," whether my lessons deserved praise or not.

In the fall of 1976, I was hired as a biology teacher at the Carden School, known for its conservative philosophy. I didn't care. I just wanted to teach. I would have my own classroom and instruct first grade through ninth. Each grade would come to my class twice a week.

The headmistress was a tall, stern woman named Mrs. Jeffs. Together with her husband, Mr. Jeffs, she had created the Carden School of Salt Lake City. They were staunch members of the John Birch Society. The dress code for the school was modest: no open-toed shoes, *toes are unattractive*; dresses must cover the knee; and hats were encouraged. My ski hats were not.

When given these instructions, I agreed they were rules I could live by. Brooke's mother, Rosemary, made me a dress out of fabric that depicted a marsh. It was a yellow cotton jersey print with cattails and dragonflies. I loved it, and wore it for the school pictures. Mrs. Jeffs found my outfit a distraction.

"It is best not to advertise one's subject by wearing it," she said.

Even so, they gave me the key to my classroom, and I immediately set out to decorate it. I purchased a window hive, complete with honeybees and a queen who had access to the outside. Their social workings would be visible to the students.

I cut out letters from green construction paper that read, BIOLOGY: THE STUDY OF LIFE. I brought in rocks and feathers and shells. Filled the shelves with field guides and all manner of books on the natural world. I created a mountain landscape on the bulletin board, which I imagined the children would populate with their own drawings of local birds, mammals, amphibians, reptiles, fish, insects, and plants. It was thrilling to create an atmosphere that I hoped would inspire students to investigate "nature."

My last gesture of the day was to write on the chalkboard, "Welcome. My name is Mrs. Williams. What do you see out the window?" I clapped my hands to get rid of the chalk dust, turned off the lights, and closed the door behind me. School would begin in two weeks. The next day, Brooke and I left for Alaska.

Fresh from Denali National Park, I returned to Carden excited to teach my first class of second graders, only to find my room completely dismantled. Vandalized? Where were the bees, the rocks, my shells? Why had the blackboard been erased and the cutout letters removed? Thirty minutes before class I walked down the hall into Mrs. Jeffs's office.

"Come in," she said. "Welcome home, Mrs. Williams. What can I do for you?"

"Mrs. Jeffs, something terrible has happened. Everything in my room is gone."

"The best learning occurs in a clean environment, Mrs. Williams. Is there anything else we need to discuss?"

I was speechless.

"Mr. Jeffs removed the clutter. And beginning today, you will never use the word *biology* with our students."

"Excuse me?"

"The word *biology* is inappropriate for our students."

"I thought that's what I was hired to teach."

Mrs. Jeffs stood up and straightened her brown wool skirt and walked around from her large desk. "Science, Mrs. Williams. You have been hired to teach science. The word *biology* denotes sexual reproduction, and we will have none of that here at Carden." She looked over my shoulder. "I believe you have a group of students waiting for you."

And so began my first day as a teacher at Carden School in Salt Lake City.

Because I fell in love with the children, I learned to work around the eccentricities of the Jeffses. I actually admired Mrs. Jeffs's capacity to teach, especially her classes in reading and literature, which I was required to watch. Students were mesmerized by her gift of storytelling. She loved the classics and believed in reading out loud. She invited the students to imagine their own plots, anticipating what direction the author might take them. Huckleberry Finn, floating on a handmade raft down the Mississippi River with his friend Jim, might as well have been heading toward Great Salt Lake.

And when she discussed Shakespeare's play *Julius Caesar* with a class of ninth graders, they speculated on how Caesar transformed the Roman Republic into the Roman Empire. What followed was a conversation about leadership.

Literature was life, and reading became an open door to a world beyond the familiar. Students both loved her and feared her. There was a depth to her pedagogy that I never fully understood. Once, when a particular class of mine was completely out of control, I walked out of the classroom into the hall, closed the door, and leaned against it in tears. Mrs. Jeffs walked by.

"Is there a problem, Mrs. Williams?"

"No, Mrs. Jeffs."

"Just remember, your classroom is a mirror of yourself," she said, walking briskly to her office.

It was the height of the Save the Whales movement in the 1970s, and I was as enthralled as anyone by the plight of the cetaceans. I read Joan McIntyre's *Mind in the Waters: A Book to Celebrate the Consciousness of Whales and Dolphins*, published by the Sierra Club in 1975, the year Brooke and I were married.

Mimi took me on whale-watching excursions off the coast of California, where we were eye to eye with gray whales, seeing them breach, tasting salt water on our lips as the whale's fluke, so close, slapped the sea before it descended. Mimi talked about a place called Esalen, in Big Sur, where interspecies communication was taking place, including actual sex between women and dolphins. Anything was possible. The silver-gray whale pendant I wore around my neck on a cord of leather was not emblematic, but religious.

My first graders were also in love with whales. I covered the tall windows with blue paper, moved all the desks and chairs to the side, and turned off the lights.

I turned on the record player and put on Roger Payne's album *Songs of the Humpback Whale*.

We discussed how whales were threatened and how difficult it was for them to find one another in the enormity of the sea. I invited the children to lie down on the floor and close their eyes as they listened to the humpbacks' haunting, deep, sonorous cries. The children began wildly, joyously swimming around the room, not only imagining what it might be like to be a whale, but becoming one. I turned up the volume and joined them.

Suddenly the door shot open, the lights flashed on, and I heard the scratch of the needle on the record as the whale songs abruptly ended.

"What on Earth is this?" said Mrs. Jeffs.

"We are whales looking for our mates . . ." a first grader cried out, now upright on his knees.

What I remember next was being led out of the classroom by a very angry headmistress. I don't think she had me by the ear, but she might have.

I was immediately escorted to her office. She called for Mr. Jeffs through the intercom. I sat. She sat tapping her fingers on the brown leather pad engraved in gold that covered her desk. Mr. Jeffs came running into her office with his sensible shoes that never made a sound on the shiny floors.

"Yes, Mrs. Jeffs?"

Mrs. Jeffs told him of the shock she had seen, how she heard "the most terrifying sounds coming from Mrs. Williams's classroom." He looked more stunned than she did, all six feet four inches of him. They disappeared into an alcove and whispered.

When they returned, I was interrogated.

"Mrs. Williams, we have one question for you, and you had better think hard before you answer it."

There was a long pause.

"Are you an E n v i r o n m e n t a l i s t ?"

Mrs. Jeffs asked, drawing out the word, as they both stared at me.

"Yes, I am," I said.

"We thought so!" Mr. Jeffs said.

"We had our suspicions when you and Mr. Williams went to Alaska and did not carry a gun," Mrs. Jeffs added.

Mr. Jeffs leaned toward me. "Did you know that the Devil is an environmentalist?"

"No, I did not," I replied.

And I was fired.

As I got up to leave, Mr. Jeffs turned to Mrs. Jeffs and said, "But what will we tell the children if Mrs. Williams is no longer here?"

Mrs. Jeffs looked out her window for a long time. "You have a point. It would be difficult to explain. They do like her."

She looked at me. "Mrs. Williams, we know you love the children, and they obviously enjoy you. Why you had them swimming on the filthy floor calling to one another as whales is something I never want to think about again, much less see repeated." She paused, with a quick glance at Mr. Jeffs. "We will consider rehiring you on the following condition: You must never again bring your politics into a Carden classroom. The children must never know that you are an—"

"An environmentalist," I said.

"Precisely."

I promised with my own condition. "And I would ask that you not walk into my classroom unannounced."

We shook hands, and I walked back into an empty classroom, which still emanated a blue glow from the covered windows.

I taught at Carden for five years. Loved it. Loved the children and all I learned from them. In the end, Mrs. Jeffs and I respected each other. Teaching helped me find my voice through the creativity of translations. The challenge was to impart large ecological concepts to young, burgeoning minds in a language that wasn't polemical, but woven into a compelling story. My task as a teacher was to honor the integrity of fact while at the same time igniting the students' imagination. To create an atmosphere where each child felt free to explore their own questions without fear of being reprimanded was my greatest pleasure.

Rachel Carson wrote, "If a child is to keep alive his inborn sense of wonder, he needs the companionship of at least one adult who can share it, rediscovering with him the joy, excitement, and mystery of the world we live in."

What Mrs. Jeffs never realized, and I came to learn, was that a shared love of nature was the most political act of all. Finding one's voice is a process of finding one's passion. I found my voice in teaching.

My curriculum became the children's curiosity. I trusted wherever it would lead us. We played. We experimented. We drew, and we wrote about the world around us. The children brought the outside in. We watched a praying mantis prey on her mate and spin an egg sac on a stick and die from exhaustion. Her green arms were locked around what she had created. The next spring, a chain of baby mantises emerged from the egg sac. Even Mr. and Mrs. Jeffs became enthused about new life in Room 8.

One day, Lee Chouquette, a nine-year-old mathematical genius, asked if he could help me teach our class about the velocity of the solar system in relationship to an expanding and contracting universe. He saw I was struggling. The success of any teacher is to recognize what one doesn't know. Ted Major had taught me well. So a child who understood quantum physics but had never learned how to skip took our class outside to the playground and arranged us according to planetary orbits. He placed me at the center as the Sun. One child became Mercury, running very fast around me. Another child was Venus, another Earth, each one moving according to the statistics Lee had calculated in his head. He gave Saturn an extra challenge, to spin a hula hoop around her waist while still moving forward in a circle, and Pluto stood in the parking lot, never moving at all. It was a visual lesson none of us forgot and each of us internalized. When the solar system had been set in motion, Lee lay on the lawn and moved from a fetal position to a stretch, expanding and contracting. No one asked who he was or what he was doing, but clearly he had a vision.

Lee now hires himself out as a wedding DJ through his business, called Cloud 10 Entertainment. Lee Chouquette's day job is as a software engineer. The bass notes of our voice are found in what we do naturally.

XXIII

O N MY TWENTY-FIFTH BIRTHDAY my mother gave me a card. On the envelope it reads, "To My Daughter and My Dearest Friend." Inside, the card holds a pressed wild rose, framed like a stained-glass window.

September 8, 1980
Dearest Terry:

I remember someone asked me many years ago what I would want most for you as a mother, and I remember saying exactly what I felt my own parents gave to me.

I said, "I want her to value herself and know how much she has been loved."

I hope you know how very loved and appreciated you are to us . . .

Thank you for always sharing yourself with me. I love this quote on relationships: "Security in a relationship lies neither in looking back to what it was in nostalgia nor forward to what it might be in dread or anticipation, but living the present relationship and accepting it as it is now." I feel this describes what we share so well.

Terry, each woman must come of age herself— she must find her true center alone. This is such an exciting process and you will find fulfillment and self-growth the next twenty-five years. If everything is right within you, nothing that happens to you can go wrong.

My Heavenly Father must have loved me very much to have sent me a daughter and friend such as you.

All my love,
Mother

I turn the card over and read it again. Her script is beautiful in its floral nature, each letter unfolding to the next, generous and open. I always loved Mother's handwriting. It is easy to read, consistent in its thoughtfulness. Even now it reassures me. Can a type of penmanship be optimistic? I felt my mother's writing always slanted toward the positive.

My memories of my twenty-fifth birthday, however, are negative. Mother planned a surprise birthday party for me. I was told we were having only our immediate family over for cake and ice cream. This meant two parents, three brothers, my four grandparents, and Brooke.

Mimi had given me a navy blue wool suit for my birthday that came with a matching pair of Bermuda shorts. They were not my style, but I thought this would be the perfect occasion to wear them, since no one but family would be there. Let's just say I looked like a sailor whose pants had shrunk to above her knees. It didn't help that I had on a white blouse with a red, white, and blue bow tie, complete with a suit jacket. Brooke teased me mercilessly.

"This is not about me," I said. "It will please Mimi to see me wearing this for the first (and only) time on my birthday."

Mother had been worried I was depressed, perceiving that I did not know what direction my life should take. She was right. I felt like Henrietta, the caged canary we had as kids who was constantly shredding and shedding her yellow feathers by flying into the bars of the cage, trying to escape. I would make a bouquet of them, placing them against a blue sky inside a small glass jar on the windowsill of my red room. Did I have the courage to forge a path contrary to the way I had been raised and break with the traditional roles of women? When I would sit on the pews in church with other young married couples, I would become claustrophobic, needing always to sit at the edge of the row. My mind would wander. The only thing that held my attention was the clock.

It might seem silly now, but in 1980 in Utah within my community, there weren't a lot of alternative role models to emulate. I wondered if I had the strength to pursue my own education and postpone having children. When I would see infants being held in the arms of new mothers, I would count back to my last period.

Brooke and I walked into my parents' house. Everything felt normal, comfortable. The family was there, my grandparents were there, but I noticed the cake on the table seemed large, even for a chocolate cake. My brother Steve teased me about my "Buster Brown look." Mimi commented on how "darling" my outfit was, and within fifteen minutes, fifty people arrived to wish me "happy birthday." It was more than a surprise, it was a humiliation.

Aside from being caught in my sailor suit, I had to endure an evening of well-meaning tributes and an excruciating slide show titled *This Is Your Life*, followed by my pale attempt to sound grateful. What was planned to uplift my spirits made me sick. I went home and immediately threw up.

The unexpected gift was this: after seeing my life on a carousel of images, bored literally to tears, I decided, Why not do something arresting? Teaching at Carden had become intolerable the day Mrs. Jeffs decided to postpone Christmas. The children's singing of Yuletide carols was not up to her standard. She canceled the Christmas assembly until January. I applied for graduate school. Having children could wait. My desire to find my own voice in the world could not.

XXIV

CHANGING WOMAN was impregnated by The Sun and gave birth to The Twins, Monster Slayer and Child of the Water. In the Navajo pantheon, this is the holy family I met when I traveled to the Four Corners in the American Southwest.

Geology became genealogy. Lava fields became the congealed blood of demons who died on these battlefields, brought down by Monster Slayer to save the People. Shiprock became Winged Rock, much more than a remnant plug of a volcano. The morphology of plants, animals, rocks, and rivers is not answered simply by science but constitutes and contributes to the cosmology of the people who inhabit a place. And it is spiritual.

Earth. Mother. Goddess. In every culture the voice of the Feminine emerges from the land itself. We clothe her as Eve or Isis or Demeter. In the desert, she appears as Changing Woman. She can shift shapes like the wind and cut through stone with her voice like water. And when she approaches us with her open hands carrying offerings of white shells in arid country, she reminds us that there was a time before drought when ancient seas covered the desert. She is not to be classified. She is not to be controlled. She is the one who gathers seeds and plants them in the sand as dreams and calls forth rain. She is the one who embodies the Moon, honoring the cyclic nature of life. And it is Changing Woman who is honored in the ceremony of first blood. Kinaaldá is her ritual, initiating each Navajo girl into womanhood. I wish someone had told me when I was young that it was not happiness I could count on, but change.

The Diné mentored me in story. When I saw a coiled basket in the desert, it uncoiled like a snake. When I found a flicker feather caught between the fingers of sage, its burned red shaft spoke to the bravery of this bird who flew directly toward the Sun to retrieve fire for the People. And when I saw Mountain Lion move across the redrock cliffs like melted butter, it was not a catamount, but powerful medicine that asked for the sprinkling of corn pollen on the place where one is graced by presence.

The question *What stories do we tell that evoke a sense of place?* became my obsession. Through the generosity of the Diné, I heard how voice finds its greatest amplification through story.

For many years, I wandered through the desert in search of a narrative that was not mine. I did not feel I belonged here. I was borrowing a landscape until I found my own. But when I stopped searching and settled into the erosional peace of the redrock desert, I found myself quietly held by an immensity I could not name. I took off my clothes and lay on my back in a dry arroyo and allowed the heat absorbed into the pink sand to enter every cell in my body. I closed my eyes and became simply another breathing presence on the planet.

XXV

"W HY ARE WE HERE?"

"To keep the story going."

"What is the story?"

"The story is Life."

Brooke and I were having this conversation on the banks of the Colorado River as we were reading out loud *The Story of My Heart* by Richard Jefferies, a gem of a book published in 1883.

"Naked mind confronts Naked Earth . . . Give me the deepest soul-life."

It is a conversation we have never stopped having with each other. How do we give voice to creation?

Before Brooke and I were married in the Salt Lake Temple, we made personal vows in a ceremony prior to our wedding day, also within the temple, with our parents present as witnesses. In Mormon theology this is called "taking out one's endowments." It is a sacred rite of passage.

What I will share is this: Men sit on one side of the room and women sit on the other. Holy instructions are given. The story of Adam and Eve is recounted. Brooke and I were picked to represent the First Couple in the Garden of Eden. Honored to be chosen, we stood before the congregation as we stood in for Adam and Eve. Eve was a virgin; so was I. As I listened to this biblical text being read on the eve of my marriage, the only word inhabiting my mind was *fuck*. I blushed. This was not a word within my vocabulary as a chaste nineteen-year-old woman. Shocked by the betrayal of my own imagination, I tried to clear my thoughts, keep my countenance clean and pure. But the word kept pressing on me, *fuck, fuck*, a word I had never spoken out loud. I turned a deeper shade of red. Brooke began smiling, wondering why I kept blushing.

Embarrassed? Flushed with a fever? I was experiencing both. Once again, between being asked to repeat certain words, this four-letter word kept announcing itself in the most holy of moments, pulling my attention away from the marriage of Adam and Eve to the allure of the seductive snake. I tried to stay focused on Brooke as we held each other's hands. *Fuck, fuck, fuck*. The dance between the sacred and the profane only became more heated.

In this very public moment I was privately struggling with my own demon. "In the beginning was the Word." Nobody warned me about which one.

I could never make my mind behave. When I was a child, Mimi and I listened to music together. "Relax. Just let your mind go blank," she would say. It never happened. Her request for an empty mind only created a rebellious one that filled quickly. I think it was in those moments, listening to her favorite composers, Beethoven and Bach, who would become mine, that I came to recognize my unruly imagination. I would always create my own accompanying narrative.

When Mimi gave me the book *Creation Myths* by Marie-Louise von Franz, I didn't understand it as a subversive text. I had been taught that the story of Adam and Eve was a biblical primer on good and evil and the consequences of following one's own appetite. To disobey God was to be cast out of the Garden of Eden and face "sorrow in your loins for all your remaining days." What I came to appreciate was how the transgression of Eve was an act of courage that led us out of the garden into the wilderness. Who wants to be a goddess when we can be human? Perfection is a flaw disguised as control. The moment Eve bit into the apple, her eyes opened and she became free. She exposed the truth of what every woman knows: to find our sovereign voice often requires a betrayal. We just have to make certain we do not betray ourselves. For a woman or a man to speak from the truth of their heart is to break taboo. The mask is removed. The snake who tempted Eve to eat the forbidden fruit was not the Devil, but her own instinctive nature saying, *Honor your hunger and feed yourself.*

Devil spelled backward is Lived.

Reading has not only changed my life but saved it. The right books picked at the right times—especially the one that scares us, threatens to undermine all we have been told, the one that contains forbidden thoughts—these are the books that become Eve's apples.

"An awakening toward consciousness is identical with the creation of the world . . . Creation myths are the deepest and most important of all myths. In many primitive religions, the telling of the creation myth forms an essential teaching in the ritual of initiation," writes von Franz.

My Mother's Journals are a creation myth.

I am writing the creation story of my own voice through the blank pages my mother has bequeathed to me. Transgression is transmission.

XXVI

M Y SENSUALITY became my sexuality when Brooke first saw me undress, his eyes directing his hands slowly moving across my breasts in twilight. We were at the Bear River Bird Refuge, lying in the spring grasses, avocets flying over us. On our backs, looking up. Brooke leaned over and kissed me. We never closed our eyes as we entered our own private geography of taste and touch and time. I remember the red-winged blackbirds singing as we mapped each other's bodies. Tongue on flesh, we were writing the secret words between lovers.

Gustave Courbet painted *L'Origine du monde* as a challenge to what we know but choose not to reveal. His is an intimate, sensual portrait of a woman's genitalia after lovemaking, swollen and glistening; her legs are open, one breast barely exposed beneath a white sleeping gown. The private becomes public. Courbet's personal gaze celebrates the unseen seen. It now hangs at the Musée d'Orsay in Paris, not as something pornographic, but revelatory.

This painting hung for years in Jacques Lacan's country house behind a sliding wooden door, hidden. Art critics have called it "a full-frontal legs-spread record of a woman's torso from her breasts to her thighs . . . Courbet's unblinking portrait for a Turkish diplomat painted in 1866." But that is far too clinical.

When I stood before her, this unknown known woman in repose, I saw myself, my mother, my grandmother, a woman revealed lovingly by a man's hand and eye, rendered in oil, barely 18 by 21 inches on a rectangular canvas. I wept. I wept at the beauty of naming it so clearly. *Origin of the World*. We come into this world through women, a woman who is spent, broken open, in awe. No wonder women have been feared and worshipped ever since man first saw the crowning of a human head here, legs spread, a brushstroke of light.

We are Fire. We are Water. We are Earth. We are Air.

We are all things elemental.

The world begins with yes.

Changing Women. We begin again like the Moon. We can no longer deny the destiny that is ours by becoming women who wait—waiting to love, waiting to speak, waiting to act. This is not patience, but pathology. We are sensual, sexual beings, intrinsically bound to both Heaven and Earth, our bodies a hologram. In our withholding of power, we abrogate power, and that creates war.

The Australian poet Judith Wright says, "Our dream was the wrong dream, our strength was the wrong strength . . . Wounded we cross the desert's emptiness, and must be false to what would make us whole."

XXVII

M Y BODY IS MY COMPASS, and it does not lie. As women, we are quiet about our personal lives, especially when it comes to sex. We are quiet because there is a history of abuse and harm committed toward those who tell the truth. Marriages are shattered. Families are broken. Judgments are rendered. The woman stands alone. Our stories live underground.

Muriel Rukeyser asked the question "What would happen if one woman told the truth about her life? The world would split open."

The world is splitting open.

On October 16, 1916, Margaret Sanger opened the first family planning and birth control center on 46 Amboy Street in the Brownsville neighborhood of Brooklyn. Nine days later it was raided by police. Margaret Sanger, the leader of the modern-day birth control movement, spent thirty days in prison. She would be arrested seven more times in her eighty-seven years of living, for speaking out on behalf of a woman's right to birth control and the privacy of her own body.

H. G. Wells stated at a 1931 dinner speech in Margaret Sanger's honor, "The movement she started will grow to be, a hundred years from now, the most influential of all time in controlling man's destiny on earth."

When we were children, we visited Mother in the hospital. We were told she was having "corrective surgery." Later I learned she made the decision to have her tubes tied, not a common practice among her peers. "Freedom," she said.

Birth control gave me my voice. It is perhaps the only thing in my life about which I have been utterly responsible. I have never had an abortion, but I was grateful to have that choice before me. I was a senior at Highland High School in 1973, when the landmark case *Roe v. Wade* was decided in the Supreme Court. It was a decision that gave us confidence as young women entering sexual maturity that we did have control over our own bodies.

No woman terminates a pregnancy easily. No one who has ever felt life inside her can negate that power. It is never a decision made lightly, without love or pain or a prayer toward forgiveness.

Because what every woman knows each month when she bleeds is, *I am not pregnant.* Because what every woman understands each time she makes love is, *Life could be in the making now.* Which is why when a woman allows a man to enter her, it is not just a physical act, but an act of surrendering to the possibility that her life may no longer be hers alone. Because until she bleeds, she will check her womb every day for the stirrings of life. Because until she bleeds, she wonders if her life will be one or two or three. Because until she bleeds, she imagines every possibility from pleasure to pain to birth to death and how she will do what she needs to do, and until she bleeds, she will worry endlessly, until she bleeds.

If a man knew what a woman never forgets, he would love her differently.

No, I have never had an abortion, but I know the tenderness of many women who have. It is much more common than we choose to admit. We have gone underground. This is the conversation we are not having. The abortions we have experienced are an intrinsic part of who we are and what we have become. And it is deeply private. Just recently I learned that three of my closest friends have had abortions. It is not something we ever discussed. One involved a genetic disease, another was a situation that would have imperiled her marriage, and another was a pregnancy in college that would have changed the course of the woman's life. We make a choice. This is our spiritual and legal right in the United States of America. We deserve to make this choice without the judgments of others.

There is nothing abstract about giving birth. There is nothing more sobering than for a woman to place her hands on her belly and wonder what is the right thing to do. It is always about love. It is never done lightly. And there is nothing more demeaning to women than to have a man, especially a man we don't know, define the laws that will govern our milk and blood.

Milk and *blood*.

Why these two words?

Because milk—as in cow as in breast as in semen as in any substance that nurtures and nourishes at once—is at the heart of pleasure. Because we drink deeply. Because we drink deeply out of need and desire.

Because blood, as in flow as in menses as in moon as in cycle, means *I am not pregnant*. Because what every woman understands each time she makes love is, *Life could be in the making now*. Which is why, when a woman allows a man to enter her, it is not just a physical act, but a spiritual one.

Milk and blood.

Because milk is what we desired first. Because blood is what flows through our working heart. Milk and blood. Men and women. Pleasure and pain. Love is to life what life is to death. And so we risk everything trying to touch the ineffable by touching each other. Over and over. Again and again. With little control, we lose our minds as we lose ourselves in fire.

If a man knew what a woman never forgets, he would love her differently.

What a woman never forgets is when she allows a man to make love to her, she enters a pact with angels that should a child be conceived in that moment, she holds the life of another. A man can come and go, he pulls out and walks away. But a woman stays and remains tender. She wants to be held. She wants to talk. She wants to revisit that motion made inside her because in the lovemaking, a woman is remade— because until she bleeds, she knows that man is the father of her child whether she ever tells him or not. Because until she bleeds, her body has been rearranged through his ecstasy and hers, which will now become theirs. Because until she bleeds, *repeat it again*, she will check her womb every day for the stirrings of life. Because until she bleeds, she wonders if her life will be one or two or three. *Repeat and repeat*, because until she bleeds, she imagines every possibility from pleasure to pain to birth to death and how she will do what she needs to do, and until she bleeds, she will worry endlessly, until she bleeds.

Milk and blood live together.

XXVIII

I DIDN'T WANT Mother to come. Not yet. I was working as an intern at the American Museum of Natural History in New York. I needed to live my own life and not be inhabited by hers. But when she came to visit, we transformed ourselves into doves cooing and coddling each other as we walked and talked in the park for hours. Mother and I adapted to each other anywhere and everywhere each time we were together.

I didn't want her to go. *Please stay.* She was my witness to what I loved. When we toured the museum, I made her lie on her back and look up at the blue whale suspended from the blue ceiling. When we went to the Museum of Modern Art, we sat before Monet's *Water Lilies* watching the light shift and the colors deepen. And when we saw Lillian Hellman's play *The Little Foxes*, starring Elizabeth Taylor, Mother insisted we leave early to sit at Sardi's, where her favorite actress (whose birthday she shared) dined after each performance. Elizabeth Taylor arrived right on cue and walked through the front door in her purple caftan and jewels. Mother was waiting for her. Sitting on the lounge with her legs crossed, she coyly extended her leg. Elizabeth Taylor tripped on my mother's foot.

"Forgive me," the actress said.

"Not at all—" Mother replied. "You were magnificent tonight."

"Thank you, you are very kind."

We were seated among the glitterati.

On our way back to the brownstone where I was living, we walked through the theater district, dazzled by the neon lights. The full moon hanging between skyscrapers was almost indistinguishable from the floodlights promoting new shows on Broadway.

"What's the difference between Elizabeth Taylor and Saturn?" I asked Mother.

"Tell me," she said, smiling.

"Elizabeth Taylor has more rings."

Mother left me a letter with a beautiful glass globe that was painted with golden waves circling the orb like the script of water.

April 17, 1983
New York City

Dearest Terry,
When I walked into this stationery shop today, you seemed to be in everything I saw and touched.

When I saw this paperweight, I knew there was
a connection to you. I had to buy it because of what it
represented but I didn't know what it was.

And then as we were sitting at the Museum this
afternoon watching Monet's mural, Water Lilies,
I knew the secret of the gift I was giving you.

In the center of the ball is the red lily pad,
which is you and all around you beautiful billows
of space— Never let anyone invade that part of you,
Terry. It is your creativity.

If you keep yourself centered, everything will be
balanced in your life.

Thank you for your love and friendship. You are a
precious gift to me. I can't tell you how much you are
constantly enriching my life.

I will always treasure the experience we have
shared this week in New York.

I love you so much,
Mother

XXIX

THE DREAM I had was this: A necklace of bird
beaks was placed around my neck, by whom I
could not see. "You will be going to Africa," a voice
said. And then I was handed some seeds.

Nairobi, 1985: I stood inside a large terra-cotta pot, holding on to the trunk of a ficus tree to gain some elevation and a reprieve from the crush of crowds. In the cacophony of voices at the UN Decade for Women Forum, one voice stood out. Her name was Professor Wangari Maathai.

"The problems of Africa are shadowed for the rest of the world. There is a problem here and it is deforestation," she said. "If you do not address the environmental situation you address nothing . . . And until the village people understand the problem, the problem will not be solved."

It was a voice unlike any I had heard before. She was passionate. She was commanding and she was smart. When Wangari Maathai spoke it was about doing something, something simple, something positive, something real, like planting a tree.

I listened.

"To plant a tree, you must get your hands dirty. When women go to college, so often they go back to cities for white-collar jobs and forget where they come from. It is the country people, the village people, who hold the Earth's health in their hands."

I learned how African women were carrying the environmental crisis on their backs, spending eight to ten hours a day in search of firewood for fuel so they could cook food for their families. I learned how forests were being burned for charcoal because it is more efficient than wood. As a result, the hillsides are denuded, creating chronic erosion. For the first time, I saw how environmental issues are economic issues are, ultimately, issues of social justice.

If women are suffering, children are suffering. Empower women, and you empower the community. A revolution was lit inside me. This is what I came to Africa for, unknowingly: to learn the hope of trees. I left the conference and followed Wangari into the villages of Kenya, where I witnessed for myself the work of women and what it means to grow a forest.

"We need to work a little more and talk a little less," she said to me wryly as we left Nairobi and visited a village very close to her own Kikuyu roots.

I watched women gathering seeds in the folds of their skirts, planting seeds, and tending trees on their knees, as if in prayer, their hands patting the soil to secure young saplings. Not only were they planting trees, they were nurturing possibilities. With time, the women could sell their seedlings and earn an income for their families. Hands on the Earth, restoration was being tilled.

Wangari Maathai's leadership was the pragmatism of joy. We are all uplifted by the growth of a seed. The women in the villages were finding their voice. Planting trees became more than a vocation. It was an action against oppression and a metaphor of renewal. Land health. Human health. When women work together, everyone benefits. This was my introduction to the Green Belt Movement.

Wangari Maathai became my mentor. She invited me to plant a tree for my mother in the special "Women's Forest." I returned day after day, planting more trees alongside the women who lived there, our hands stained with African seeds.

The power of Wangari Maathai's optimism fueled mine. She showed me the importance of mobilizing the public through love, while at the same time telling the hard truths of our press on the planet. Her voice not only inspired me but called me to action once I returned home.

We started the Green Belt Movement of Utah. It was a way to draw similarities between deforestation in Kenya and desertification within the Great Basin. Both landscapes were degraded by the removal of vegetation: in Africa, the cutting of trees; in the American Southwest, overgrazing by cattle. And in both situations valuable topsoil was disappearing through erosion. I engaged Mormon women in the Relief Society, an organization within the LDS Church that exists for service and sisterhood. We could collaborate between continents. I gave hundreds of talks in Relief Societies and book groups across the state, retelling the story of deforestation and Wangari Maathai's efforts to plant trees village by village, to ease the burden and oppression of women while also taking care of the Earth.

"The issue is fragmentation," Professor Maathai said. "We must look at the whole. The minute we fall for fragmentation we subvert the work of women."

I was simply passing on what I had witnessed in Kenya to the women in Utah, my own home ground, and inviting them to help. For ten dollars, a woman could purchase a tree in the name of a woman she loves. We had certificates designed and printed. It was a campaign to educate and engage. Mother and Mimi and Lettie were among the first to enroll.

Brooke's father was moved by the effort. He took me to lunch. I asked him, as a man of respect and rank within the hierarchy of the Church, if he would help by introducing me to one of the apostles, a friend of his who could make this fund-raising venture among local women expand worldwide. I knew what this could mean to the Green Belt Movement in Kenya. Nobody can organize like the Mormons. He said he would make the call for me to make my case before one of the elders in power. But there was a catch.

"You know what I have promised to do for you. Now here is what you can do for me. Promise me you will bring Brooke back into the Church, and never say we had this conversation."

I was speechless. I thought about the women in Kenya struggling to find their independence. I thought about Wangari Maathai and her unflinching ferocity in the face of institutional power. What would she do?

I sat in the center of a very long silence in the middle of our lunch. It seemed like such a simple proposition.

"I can't make that promise," I said to my father-in-law, whom I love.

My father-in-law unknowingly had forced the issue of integrity. Mine. I realized I couldn't have it both ways—use the Mormon Church's influence for what I wanted with my father-in-law's help, yet be unwilling to help him with what he wanted most, for his son to attend Church. It was a Faustian bargain. Brooke was his own sovereign, and so was I. The restriction I would be under as a Mormon woman asked to remain silent would undermine whatever good I was trying to accomplish for Kenyan women. My compromise would become theirs in principle.

Why is it that the tips of the bird beaks are burnt?
—Myung Mi Kim

I would raise the money myself. No strings attached.

We raised ten thousand dollars for the Green Belt Movement in Kenya. It wasn't a lot of money, but it came ten dollars at a time, one woman committing to the prosperity of another woman, freely.

Wangari Muta Maathai passed away from ovarian cancer on September 25, 2011. Through the years, we remained sisters. Her last gift to me was a woman's burden basket that I received in the mail on September 26, wrapped in a beautiful red cloth. When I once asked her what she had learned from planting trees, she said, "Patience."

The Green Belt Movement has planted more than forty-three million trees. Not one tree was sacrificed for her coffin. Kenyan women, with her children, Waweru, Wanjira, and Muta, buried her in a casket made from woven water hyacinths.

When I learned of her death, I was stunned. People like Wangari don't die, that's how intractable and resilient she was to me. We are never ready to lose those we love, especially a world soul like Wangari. I walked outside, knelt on the ground, and sent prayers of gratitude to her spirit. My tears became rain until a ruby-throated hummingbird hovered directly in front of me before my words were finished. I looked up and smiled. Of course, it was a hummingbird. This was Wangari's favorite bird, the one who put out a forest fire, one beak full of water at a time.

XXX

I N AUGUST cottonwood trees create a blizzard of seeds that blanket the ground. One morning I looked out the window and saw a ground squirrel draped in a coat of cotton. She was picking the cotton-seeds off her arm and eating them. Suddenly a weasel emerged and began wildly chasing the ground squirrel around the yard. Just as the weasel was about to grab the ground squirrel's neck, ensuring a quick death, the squirrel made an abrupt turn, faced the weasel, and screamed. The startled weasel jumped in the air and fell onto its back as the ground squirrel ran away.

XXXI

W HAT ARE THE CONSEQUENCES when we go against our instincts?

What are the consequences of not speaking out?

What are the consequences of guilt, shame, and doubt?

I had seen him around. He was striking, thirty-something, tanned, blond, and fit.

If you saw him once, you would remember him again. I did remember him. I felt as though I had been carrying a part of him around the edges of my attention, so when he appeared, it was as though he came to retrieve what was his.

"My name is Joseph," he said. "Would you like to go for a walk?"

"I'm working," I said. "I don't have the time."

We were both staying at a remote camp in the Sawtooth Wilderness of Idaho.

I was a teaching assistant for a field ecology course. He was doing carpentry work.

"There's a nice view up at Two Ravens at Tall Pines," he said.

I nodded, continuing to write. I knew the ridge. I didn't need to go with him.

The smell of him was smoke laced with sweat. Even in the breeze of the screened porch of the ranch house, he was a reminder of campfires in dry, hot country. Even his hands were dusty.

"I'll have you back by dinner."

I looked up.

He looked down at my moccasins. "Put on your hiking boots."

I don't know why I ignored my body's instincts, my own intuition. It had all the ingredients of an ill-fated story. Mimi had read us Andersen's and Grimm's fairy tales backward and forward. I preferred Grimm's because they were darker, scarier, more trustworthy. The boxed set of green-and-red books was tattered and worn. We all had our favorites. I always wanted to hear the story of Snow White. I liked the idea of a talking mirror and the wicked queen obsessed with her own fading beauty and threatened by her endless question, "Who is the fairest of them all?" Disguised, she tries three times to kill Snow White: first with corset laces so tight they cause her to faint, second with a poisoned comb, and third with a poisoned apple. But Snow White always manages to escape death and return to life, foiling her wicked stepmother. For me it became a love story of Snow White and the Prince, how to remain hidden yet have your powers known and survive what threatens you. The seven dwarfs seemed credible to me, growing up in a large extended family where each member provided and protected one another with their own eccentricities.

Joseph wore me down. It was easier to say yes than to say no. I put my pen and papers down, put on my hiking boots, and followed him. *How bad can this be?* I thought. *The fresh air will do me some good.*

"So you're Hathaway's assistant?"

"I am."

"What's the class?"

"Field ecology."

"How many students do you have?"

"Ten."

I didn't want to be rude, but I did not want to engage.

"How long are you here?"

"Two weeks."

Just then a great horned owl swooped in front of us. Startled by its proximity, I stopped and followed it with my eyes until I saw where it landed in a lodgepole.

I left the trail and quietly walked toward the owl. Joseph continued up the trail until he realized I was no longer behind him.

"Come on, we're not there yet," he yelled, walking back.

"I'm going to sit here for a while. I don't get a chance to be with an owl that often." And I settled into the tall yellow grasses on the hillside.

Agitated, Joseph disappeared.

The owl stayed. In its cloak of feathers it was perfectly camouflaged inside the slanted light of the pines. The owl did not move, its gaze fixed on mine, yellow eyes like flames in the forest. Who knows how much time passed in the shifting shadows of dusk?

Owls are duplicitous. They are both warning and comfort. On this occasion I refused the warning and settled into the comfort of its presence. I sank into the reverie of my own mind in the mountains. This was home for me, rarely a place of fear. Wild nature has its own rules; we were raised with them. Respect is primary. So is unpredictability. Keep your distance. Be aware. Always.

Twigs snapped; I turned around. Joseph was standing behind me wearing a loincloth, no shirt, with green Visqueen wrapped around his forehead.

"I'm cold," he said.

"I'll bet you are," I said, wondering where he had left his clothes. Even more disturbing was where he found these—or hid them—and why.

"Let's head back."

His demeanor was unsettling. He smelled of smoke. I left the owl, which meant leaving what I knew, and followed Joseph, now half naked, back to the main trail. When we reached the fork, instead of turning down, which was the way we came, Joseph stopped and said, "Let's walk up a ways until we get to Richardson Creek, and then we can work our way down. It's a shortcut to the camp, so we won't be late for dinner."

I made a calculation that continuing to follow a man who was increasingly mad was a better risk than bolting at this point. I didn't want to upset him. I can't say it was good manners, exactly, that kept me deferring to him, when every decision I was making was sabotaging good judgment, but the effort to just keep walking seemed easier than trusting what I knew. I didn't have the energy for conflict. I kept quiet. But I made a crucial error. I was forgetting the rules of fairy tales. Bad things happen to young women in the woods. I ignored the one central tenet of every fairy tale I had ever heard: Beware of the charismatic wolf in sheep's clothing. There is evil in the world. You can be tricked.

We had been walking briskly for fifteen minutes when it started getting dark. Joseph was behind me. I could hear him breathing, almost panting. I walked faster, this time with my nerves speaking to me. A steep ravine loomed large. Richardson Creek was far below. This was not the way. Every hair on my body stood up. I turned around. Joseph was standing on a large square rock. The veins in his neck were protruding. The pupils in his eyes dilated black. In what seemed to be happening in slow motion, I saw him raise a double-edged ax, now reflecting light, directly over his head, with the force of his whole body about to bear down on his target. Our eyes met. The ax was meant for me. As he lunged forward, he slipped. I ran. For a mile and a half I never looked back.

I was late for dinner. Professor Hathaway asked if everything was okay. He had been worried. I said I had just been on a long walk and had miscalculated the time.

Why did I lie? Why didn't I tell my teacher about

the terror I had just fled? I was ashamed. Perhaps it was my fault. Perhaps I had imagined the whole thing. I hadn't trusted my instincts before going with Joseph. Why should I trust them now?

That night I moved my sleeping bag out of the ranch house into a meadow far away from everyone. I felt safer outside than inside. I stared at the twinkling stars and the sweeping path of the Milky Way. But the only constellation I could see was the one in the shape of a double-edged ax. I never shut my eyes, just lay there on the ground trembling, replaying the image over and over of Joseph's dilated eyes staring through me and the throbbing terror trapped in my legs that carried me when my body turned to ice.

The next day, I wrote Brooke a long letter describing everything that had happened, including a physical description of Joseph in case I turned up missing. I transferred my burden onto Brooke. Isn't this how the story goes, the distressed maiden will be saved by the prince? If I couldn't speak, Brooke could speak for me. If something happened, Brooke could tell the tale, since I was mute. If I was wrong, I didn't want to damage Joseph's character. I put a small owl feather inside the envelope. I hiked down to the main road several miles away and flagged down a truck coming from Stanley. The man in the pickup stopped, rolled down his window, and asked if I was okay. I asked him if he would mail a letter for me. He obliged, and I handed him a couple of quarters for a stamp.

A few days later I was in the kitchen, pouring myself a cup of tea. I was finally settling back into my daily routine. I heard the screen door squeak and slam shut. I turned around, and there was Joseph, clean shaven and fully clothed. The same sickly smell of smoke corralled me into the corner. My heart was pounding. He was whispering, moving toward me slowly.

"You thought I was going to kill you, didn't you, Terry?"

All I could think of was the gleaming ax, his arms slowly rising above his head. I was too scared to speak. I just stood there, holding my cup of tea in both hands, burning my fingers, feeling the terror tingling in my legs all over again.

"Why did you run? Why did you leave me after I fell? I could have been hurt."

I heard myself evoke Brooke's name, as though it were a magical word that could shatter this spell.

"Brooke? Who is Brooke?" Joseph asked, suddenly manic, shifting his weight back and forth. "You're married? You didn't say you were married. I thought you were a virgin . . ." He became incoherent, mumbling, speaking in tongues. His blue eyes dilated to black once again as he retreated into a trance, touching my neck with his stinking fingers, his thumb pressing down slow and hard on the depression between my collarbones. He stared at me, and finally took his hand off me like a disappointment, and walked out of the pantry. No one ever saw him again.

Wolves kill sheep indiscriminately if no eye contact is made. Deer or caribou meet the eyes of the wolf and lock. In a blink, a decision is made between predator and prey. Barry Lopez calls this "the conversation of death." The animal agrees or does not agree to be taken. *No. My eyes said no. I will not be taken.* It was at that moment Joseph slipped down the side of the ravine and I ran.

In my remaining days in the Sawtooths I wanted to tell someone, anyone, what had happened. I wanted to speak. I wanted to say how scared I was, how I was almost murdered, hacked to pieces by a madman with an ax, and it wasn't my fault, but I didn't believe it. I believed it was my fault. I betrayed my instincts. My body tried to warn me. The owl tried to warn me. But I ignored them all and walked past my intuition. When one woman doesn't speak, other women get hurt. And now Joseph could be hurting another woman asleep in another wilderness.

During the last week of the field course we focused on stream studies, surveying the caddis fly and mayfly larvae living in Richardson Creek. Upstream, students started yelling frantically for us to come. We abandoned our collecting gear to see what the commotion was about.

Next to the creek, at the base of the ravine, there was a small wickiup constructed out of willows. Inside were bloody deer skulls and amulets made of bone. A small library of esoteric books on Mesoamerican cultures from Aztecs to Mayans were in orderly stacks, with sections on human sacrifice marked with pieces of torn paper. And then one of the students pulled out the double-edged ax.

I became nauseated at the sight of the weapon and excused myself. I threw up. When one student found me heaving in the bushes, she asked if she could help.

"No, thanks, just the flu."

I said nothing to no one again.

Brooke begged me to go to the police. I refused. The good Mormon girl said, "I am fine."

"Just let it go," I said.

What is the gesture of a woman's hand covering her mouth?

What is the gesture of a woman's hand covering her mouth with her eyes wide open?

———

What is the gesture of a man's thumb pressing on the heartbeat of a woman's voice while she cries through her eyes without tears?

When I hear about a young woman who has disappeared, possibly murdered, her body never found, I think about Joseph and the violence of my silence.

Mimi always said, "When a woman cries, she is closest to her most authentic self." I never cried in the Sawtooth Wilderness.

For far too long we have been seduced into walking a path that did not lead us to ourselves. For far too long we have said yes when we wanted to say no. And for far too long we have said no when we desperately wanted to say yes.

When I look in the mirror, I see a woman with secrets.

When we don't listen to our intuition, we abandon our souls. And we abandon our souls because we are afraid if we don't, others will abandon us. We've been raised to question what we know, to discount and discredit the authority of our gut.

I want to know why. I regret whenever I abandon

myself. But harboring regrets is making love to the past, and there is no movement here. It's not the lips of a prince that will save us, but our own lips speaking.

I am growing beyond my own conditioning, breaking set with what was breaking me.

XXXII

MOTHER DIED on January 16, 1987. We buried her beneath blankets of snow and the burn of frostbite. There is a melancholia to white that accompanies the blinding light of winter. Sorrow has a voice. It is the cold scream of silence turned inward.

XXXIII

WALKING IN NEW YORK after a snowstorm, I turned the corner and found a small blue wing severed at the joint lying on the wet sidewalk. Bits of muscle were still attached to the tiny bloody knob of bone. My guess, indigo bunting. I took the wing as a hostess gift to the apartment where I was staying. My friend received it as an object of uncommon beauty and placed it on the soft white tuft of the cotton plant she had displayed in a milk pitcher.

"A murderous beauty," she said.

Brooke and I were paddling down the Colorado River in Westwater Canyon in Utah. The infamous Skull Rapid awaited us. We stopped for lunch near a side canyon, where we tied up our raft. Swifts and swallows sailed above redrock walls that created the sandstone corridor where water cut through stone. Mourning doves purred. Yellow warblers were singing in willows. We sat cross-legged on the beach as Brooke took our sandwiches out of his pack.

Whirrrrrrrrrrrrrrrp!

Something shot past us like a rocket. Before I knew what had happened, Brooke was on his feet, looking over me. The corner of my eye was cut— sharp, swift, and bleeding. I touched the razor-thin line drawn by the tip of a speeding wing.

"A peregrine!" Brooke said, facing the side canyon. "Did you see that?" Then he crouched down to look at my eye, catching the long, red tear of blood with the edge of his finger. "Are you okay?"

I was fine, but had I been leaning an inch to the right instead of toward Brooke, it would have been death by falcon—a great obituary.

I am marked, scarred, my skin engraved by a

feather. Death's cry comes through a ventriloquist, whose lips you never see move until they are howling with laughter.

XXXIV

A FALCON appears on the cover of *Refuge: An Unnatural History of Family and Place*. When I first saw the proofs, the bird that graced the upper-right-hand corner was a mythical parrot. After two days of sitting with the image on my desk, I called my editor and said no such bird exists, especially near Great Salt Lake. When asked for a suggestion, I thought of the "radiant falcon" and what we don't see coming.

My mother, Mimi, and my maternal grandmother, Lettie, all died within months of one another. Cancer: breast, ovarian, cervical. Cut, mutilated, expelled. The female body ravaged. What I feared most, happened. Their deaths were a summons: Speak or die.

A decision was made. A line was crossed. I crossed that line with a pen and a pad of paper hidden in my boots. On Easter Sunday, one year after Mother's death, I committed civil disobedience at the Nevada Test Site. Arrested. Here, then in 1988, nuclear bombs were still being detonated in the desert, an experiment the American government had already performed. They knew it worked. The atomic bombs dropped on Hiroshima and Nagasaki by the United States on August 6 and August 9, 1945, successfully ended World War II. But evidently the fact that tens of thousands of people were vaporized in a great and ghostly flash was not the evidence they were looking for—they needed proof from their own citizens. My family and I are among the loyal citizens known as "downwinders."

Gesture has a voice. I found the gravity of my own words through the death of Mother and Mimi. This is the brutal irony of my life.

Here were my declarative sentences: *"I will write—I will take my anger and turn it into sacred rage. From their deaths, I must make meaning."*

There was no field guide. There was no map. I was free to improvise.

Mythmaking is the evolutionary enterprise of translating truths.

My Mother's Journal's are paper cranes.

"*I belong to a Clan of One-breasted Women.*" These words flew out of my mind after a friend simply asked, "How are you?" I could not know then what I know now, that this image allowed me to see the women in my family as warriors, not victims of breast cancer. Twenty-two years later, these words, this image, "When Women Were Birds," came to me in a dream without explanation.

Were we?

Are we still?

Or are we in motion, never to be caught? We remain elusive by choice.

"I am a woman with wings," I once wrote and will revise these words again. "I am a woman with wings dancing with other women with wings."

In a voiced community, we all flourish.

I revisit these moments in *Refuge* not as a repeat of memory, but as a reminder of how we evolve in time and place. The courage to continue before the face of despair is the recognition that in those eyes of darkness we find our own night vision. Women blessed with death-eyes are fearless.

XXXV

THERE IS A PHOTOGRAPH of my mother. She is standing on a boat on Jackson Lake with the Tetons behind her. She is wearing a checkered shirt with pearl buttons and a Levi's jacket, a bit too large. The wind must have been blowing, because she is wearing a scarf tied beneath her chin. A lock of hair has escaped confinement, creating a curl on her forehead; another flies to the side. Her eyes are searing. Her nose, straight. Her mouth is neither smile nor frown. Mother is strong. She is looking at me. I wonder what she sees.

Thirteen Ways of Looking at a Blackbird

I do not know which to prefer,
The beauty of inflections
Or the beauty of innuendoes,

The blackbird whistling
Or just after.
                    —Wallace Stevens

My Mother's Journals are "just after."

XXXVI

IN MORMON CULTURE, there is a saying, "I would walk across the plains with you."

The translation is simple: You are tough. You are reliable. You can carry your own weight. Our aunt Bea was one of those individuals, made of good pioneer stock.

Beatrice Romney Berg was my mother's aunt, my grandmother's sister, the second daughter of Vilate Lee Romney and Park Romney, who sought refuge in Mexico from the persecution associated with polygamy. In 1890 the Mormon Church issued a manifesto declaring the end of plural marriage as a sanctioned religious practice. Although polygamy was illegal in Mexico, it was still commonly practiced there among Latter-Day Saints without the same scrutiny they would find in the United States.

The family story goes like this: The Romney men were armed and ready for the arrival of Pancho Villa and his "Villistas," who were heading toward the Mormon settlement in Colonia Dublán in the region of Chihuahua. The Mexican Revolution had begun.

It was 1911. My great-grandmother Vilate was preparing dinner. Word arrived they must leave immediately. Expectant with her second child, she grabbed her baby, Lettie, barely two years old, tied her around her pregnant belly, and fled on horseback. She crossed the border with other men and women. Once in El Paso, the renegade Mormons were considered refugees. They were corralled and cornered like cattle until the United States of America decided what to do with them.

My great-grandmother told me they abandoned their homes so quickly, she left a cake baking in the oven.

What is true and what is imagined?

What is true is that Aunt Bea was born back in Utah, where the family returned after the government had given them a one-way ticket to the town of their choice. They chose Cornish, Utah, and my great-grandparents farmed sugar beets. My great-grandfather, Park Romney, was ordained as a Mormon patriarch whose job it was to hand down personalized blessings from God.

Mother's patriarchal blessing was given to her by her grandfather when she was twelve years old. He called her his little songbird.

My patriarchal blessing was given to me when I was seventeen years old, after I had graduated from high school. The line from my blessing that I still carry with me is this: "No truth will be revealed to you that will be in conflict with the truth of God." I believed this, still do, and have incorporated it into my personal theology. Who is to say this encouragement to seek questions didn't open the door for my own religious inquiry that would include the spiritual wisdom of feathers and fur?

You know you are a Mormon when you've had a family reunion and the size of your town doubles, so they say. A family reunion was scheduled at Aunt Bea's home in Salt Lake City. Mother and my grandmother Lettie had passed away within two years of each other. Bea was now the matriarch of the Romney clan. Under obligation by my own guilt to attend, I went. I was in the middle of writing and did not want to go anywhere, much less face my kin, who were in the middle of childbearing and child rearing. Creating a book was not a legitimate pregnancy.

I rang the doorbell. Aunt Bea opened the door. Would you believe me if I told you she seemed six feet three without heels? I did adore her, her booming voice, the assurance of her carriage.

"Come in—come in—" she said. "Everyone is here. Darling Terry, we are so happy you came."

The charming quality of the Romney women is their outward attention to the one they are speaking to, and I was her focus. "And tell me what you are up to. You are always doing the most interesting things—studying Indians, are you?" Aunt Bea asked. "I miss Lettie. She always kept us informed of your whereabouts."

I told her I was writing a book.

"A book? On what?"

"On Mother—"

It was here I saw her smile falter, just slightly. "On Diane?"

And then I made the mistake of saying too much. "I'm writing a book on the rise of Great Salt Lake and Mother's death."

"Well, do come in and let's get you some food." She looked at me, a quick glance at my flat stomach, and we moved into the living room, filled with the hum of relatives, many I had not seen in months, if not years. I was happy to see them.

Even so, I didn't stay long. I was disturbed. As I drove home, all my thoughts became present tense: *Maybe I really am crazy. Maybe there really is nothing to connect a flooding Great Salt Lake, a drowning bird refuge, and my mother's death from ovarian cancer.*

Once in the driveway, I remembered Brooke was

out of town. I was alone—haunted by my own thoughts, hunted by my own fears. Scared. Scarred. Inside, I put my keys down in a place where I would inevitably forget them, turned on the lights, and sank into the couch.

That night in bed I couldn't stop my mind from racing. I couldn't sleep. I got up and drew a map.

There was a childhood easel buried in our basement. It still had sheets of manila paper clipped to the board. I brought it upstairs.

With two markers in hand I scribbled the various subjects I was working with on either side of the paper:

Great Salt Lake	Mother
Bear River Bird Refuge	Family
Flood	Cancer
Division of Wildlife Resources	Mormon Church

I circled both lists. Nothing connected them. And then I realized what brought these seemingly unrelated worlds together was the narrator. So I wrote "TTW" below, circled it, and then drew two lines from each of the two circles above, connecting them all together. I stood back and stared. Suddenly I realized I wasn't crazy. Before me was a map of the female reproductive system.

I gathered my manuscript and quickly began

shuffling it into two stacks of paper: Mother, Mother, Mother; bird refuge, refuge, refuge. I grabbed the pile that had to do with Mother, tucked my nightgown into my Levi's, pulled on my cowboy boots, and tore down the canyon. I drove to the nearest Kinko's and handed half of my book to the young woman behind the counter.

"Would you mind printing this on the brightest paper possible?"

"It will be difficult to read," she said.

"That's okay."

"Turquoise?"

"Perfect."

And then I waited, watching the clock. I didn't realize it was after two in the morning. It was just the shopgirl and me.

Suddenly the door opened, and in walked a man in worse shape than I was.

It was the poet Mark Strand. We were friends. I was praying my neon-colored manuscript would not be delivered just now.

"What are you doing here?" he asked.

"Mark, are there days you feel like you cannot write one more word?" At that moment he could have slain me. All my defenses were down.

"Every single day." He didn't even notice my blue pages as he handed the young woman his white ones.

Once home with my turquoise stack, I reshuffled the manuscript, putting the pages back in order. Where there was too much blue, I realized it was too intense. Too much white, too many birds. My task was to create a light blue manuscript that gracefully wove together two parallel stories into one coherent book.

Utter: absolute, completely—to make words.

Soul utterance: to speak through our vulnerability with strength.

XXXVII

To the owl who cries at dawn: I ask you why—*why now*—when night is surrendering to light? Why not sound your haunting call as the Sun begins to set, when we are wrapped in shawls of shadows, expecting to disappear into darkness? Why not then, so we can listen to you who are crying—*There is nothing we can do*—I ask you now, why do you save your voice for the moment of awakening? Because when you call to me on the edge of dreams, I want to linger in the comfort of sleep, cling to my covers—*sleep, sleep, sleep*—where even a chimera feels like a safer presence than you who calls me forward with crepuscular courage to say, *Rise—now—soon.*

My Mother's Journals are a koan.

My Mother's Journals are a meditation.

My Mother's Journals are a stand of lotus blossoms,
unfolding.

XXXVIII

NOT THE LOTUS WITHOUT THE MUD. Cancer. So much cancer. *Nine women in my family have all had mastectomies, and seven are dead.* Mimi died on June 27, 1989. I awoke the next day to a summer from which all the color had been drained. It was not a world of black and white, but gray.

Even at eighty-four years of age, after a long and fecund life, she left too soon.

I could not get out of bed. I could not get on with my life. And when I did leave the house, I sat for hours by a man-made pond in a man-made park, with domesticated ducks floating on a mirror of water. I stared into nothing. Nothing mattered. I was paralyzed. Brooke told me walking would help.

Every day, I walked. It was not a meditation, but survival, one foot in front of the other, with my eyes focused down, trying to stay steady.

The moss in Owl Canyon was so dry it could not even accept the water we poured on it. Instead, the small beads simply rolled off like tears in the desert. I had no idea of the depth of the drought in our country.

We continued to walk up the serpentine canyon on the edge of the Colorado River in Utah. Cracked, dried mud was the least of what we saw. Tadpoles trying to become frogs before the two-feet-by-two-feet pool evaporated. Swifts pulled down from the air to drink from the last drops of a once-trustworthy spring. Penstemons barely able to send out shoots of green could not overcome last fall's skeletons, now wind rattles. Everywhere we turned, there was a sense of a world parched—and of penury.

A maroon ring had formed around one of the dried pools, peculiar and beautiful. My friend Laura Kamala, a biologist, said simply, "Algae."

We knelt to touch it. The maroon algae turned orange, as if by magic. We rubbed it again gently, discovering that the greater the agitation, the more vibrant the color. It was an orange displaced within my own spectrum of experience. The color was more radiance than pigment. It was carotene alive on my fingers.

Is this what early desert dwellers knew as they painted their histories on the red-rock walls?

I painted a circle of orange in the palm of my left hand and placed my other hand against it in prayer. When I opened my hands, one circle became two. Laura created a spiral on her hands and drew a cross on each of her feet. I marked my forehead, throat, between my breasts, down to my navel, to the tops of my feet, and then placed one orange dot on the back of my neck.

Ritual creates its own logic.

Lizards drew near with turquoise bellies, pumping themselves up and down, up and down, and I wondered what it is in times of drought that creates this kind of abundance. There is an unknown palette before us. The algae were flourishing in the midst of struggle, begging to be used. Agitation gives birth to creation.

We walked down the canyon, back toward our home, opening our hands to sage, registering the shock of orange against its pale silver-blue. The sage awakened in concert with orange. Salt brush and rabbitbrush also intensified, their small, feathery leaves shimmering in the heat. We placed our palms as a backdrop against everything still alive in the drought of the desert and watched its character come forth.

What to name this color?

Once home, I stood outside before the crumbling, eroded landscape. The orange flame we had ignited was ablaze in our garden of globe mallow, and there it was again, orange wings fluttering against blue, the penultimate orange of monarchs.

Mimi took up painting toward the end of her life, something she had always wanted to pursue. One of her last canvases was titled *Self Portrait*. She painted a house wren perched on her finger pointing the way.

XXXIX

THE WILDERNESS SOCIETY has a distinguished history in conservation. Mardy Murie, the wife of Olaus Murie—the Wilderness Society's first president—and a conservationist in her own right, was a close friend and mentor of mine beginning with my days at the Teton Science School. The 1964 Wilderness Act was drafted on their front porch at the Murie Ranch inside Grand Teton National Park. As president of the Wilderness Society in 1950, Olaus lobbied successfully to prevent large federal dam projects within Glacier National Park and Dinosaur National Monument. He enlisted the writer Wallace Stegner to join him in creating the book *This Is Dinosaur* as a literary tool for advocacy.

Wallace Stegner was a member of the Wilderness Society's Governing Council, as was Arnie Bolle, the great reformer of forest policy, and Charles Wilkinson, a law professor at the University of Colorado, an expert on western water policy and Indian law. There were twenty-six members on the Governing Council, and two of them were women: Alice M. Rivlin, deputy director of the Office of Management and Budget in the Clinton administration, and Jane H. Yarn, a conservationist from Georgia. At Mardy's urging, I accepted the invitation to join them.

The first year I served on the Governing Council of the Wilderness Society, I never opened my mouth. I listened. I listened to the men pontificate on public-lands policy. They argued. They debated. They made recommendations. It was impressive. Alice Rivlin was central to any conversation about finances and budgetary considerations. Jane Yarn, always gracious, would contribute her knowledge, but usually only when southern land issues arose.

During one of the meeting breaks I left the room to go for a quick walk outside. I walked toward the elevator, where Alice Rivlin was standing. She pushed the down button. The doors opened. We stepped inside. We both stared at the closed doors as the elevator descended.

"Do you have a voice?" she asked, looking ahead at the panels of buttons.

"Yes," I answered.

"It would be nice to hear it—" The elevator doors opened, and she briskly disappeared.

The second year I served on the Governing Council, I did speak. I took Alice Rivlin at her word and began contributing to the conversation. I noticed two things. First, when I asked a question or offered a comment, there would be a slight pause, and then the discussion would continue with no reference to what I had just said. I felt invisible, heard only in the context of offering a moment of poetic insight. Peripheral.

Second, I did not have the same information that everyone else around the table seemed to have. I read all the materials twice. I studied the issues with the accompanying proposals, and still I was missing key pieces of the discussion. I couldn't figure it out.

After one of the meetings, one of the men invited me to have drinks with some of the other members of the Council. I accepted. It was here I learned what everyone else knew. Policy is decided outside the boardroom. The meeting itself is a formality.

I had been reading *The Tongue Snatchers*, by the French writer Claudine Herrmann. She focuses on the French verb *voler*, which means "to fly" or "to steal," the two paths traditionally available to women when we speak. We either flee and disappear or steal, adopt, and adapt to the dominant language of men, often at our own expense. Herrmann offers another route, that of the "Mother Tongue," the voice with an authentic vernacular akin to our experiences, fierce and compassionate at once; the voice as a knife that can slice, carve, or cut, shape, sculpt, or stab.

I arrived early for the next day's meeting. No one was there. I placed a copy of *The Tongue Snatchers* in the middle of the table. The image of a woman screaming, her tongue stretched out, and an anonymous hand wielding a knife to cut it out might be thought-provoking. Ben Shahn's cover art of a woman in flight with her mouth wide open is disturbing. I thought if the feminine voice (for lack of a better term) continues to be eclipsed, every aspect of virile thinking will be emblazoned across the face of the Earth at all our peril. I was ready for a discussion.

It never happened.

The council members arrived. The men (Alice was not at that particular meeting, nor was Jane) took their seats, and the business of wilderness resumed. Not one word about the title, the image, or why such a book suddenly appeared as a centerpiece for the roundtable of the Wilderness Society. As Adrienne Rich writes, "The drive to connect, the dream of a common language," was ignored.

During my third year on the Governing Council I decided to infiltrate. I listened. I spoke. I lobbied behind the scenes, and I went to the bar with the men afterward. But a strange thing began to happen. The conversations became more about power and less about land. The discussions among ourselves centered around the internal politics of the organization rather than the politics of wildlands. Instead of talking about whether or not there should be cattle grazing in wilderness, we were discussing real estate, how much rent we should be paying, and the importance of positioning ourselves in a posh neighborhood.

At every meeting I kept wondering why we weren't being more forceful against George H. W. Bush's environmental policies, especially the oil and gas leases on western public lands. Access to politicians seemed more important than principles. A compromised wilderness bill was better than no wilderness bill at all. The largest donors had the largest say. I witnessed the shadow dance among conservation, corporations, and Congress that has everything to do with money and power. I was becoming part of that shadow dance as I caught my reflection in the tinted windows of the black town car I was riding in with two other members of the Council on our way back to the airport.

The fourth year, I quit. I couldn't reconcile the split within myself between conviction and compromise. Whatever gains I had made politically, I had lost personally. I realized I was a writer, not a politician, and certainly not a professional conservationist.

The buzz of Washington was exciting, but I collapsed when I returned home, depleted and despondent over what we were giving away. For me, what was real was the sweet smell of sage after rain in the desert, not lunch with a senator.

I went to Washington because I loved public lands. I went to Washington because I thought I could make a difference. I went because I had been asked to join an organization that I respected at a time when I needed to be coaxed back into the world I had withdrawn from. I cannot count the times my heart was broken, my dreams dashed, and my adrenaline spiked and drained. I didn't know how to be objective about Utah wilderness. I didn't know how to protect only part of the Arctic National Wildlife Refuge, and not all of it. And I never understood why withholding information or resources, meaning money, from other conservation organizations to protect one's own interests—meaning territory—was a strategy, not an outrage. I only knew how to advocate for what I loved.

I did not have the stomach for Washington politics. I had to face myself and the truth of my passions: all things wild, including words, words that could not be tamed, words that if cut would bleed, not words cautiously rendered, dressed up, and disguised as an interest in wilderness. Politics is a game of power and cunning. Compromise, though necessary, is not in my medicine bundle. We have already compromised too much.

I heard my voice as extreme.

XL

SOMETHING will have gone out of us as a people if we ever let the remaining wilderness be destroyed . . ." Wallace Stegner wrote in his "Wilderness Letter." "We simply need that wild country available to us, even if we never do more than drive to its edge and look in."

There was a debate among the Governing Council: Should we publicly denounce Secretary of the Interior Manuel Luhan's latest environmental policies by taking out a full-page ad in *The New York Times*, or work behind the scenes, influencing members of Congress who had access to President George H. W. Bush? The Council was split down the middle.

It was decided that Wally, in his wisdom, would be the tiebreaker. The question posed: Should we be stronger in our public response to the Bush administration or more strategic in our private one? Charles Wilkinson and I were drafted by the council to write something for *The New York Times* should we choose the more radical route. We took the declaration to Stegner at his home in Palo Alto.

"Let's hear it—" Wally said after he had been briefed about the divide and dilemma of the Governing Council. We had just finished a long, lovely lunch with his wife, Mary, on their porch overlooking the soft yellowed hills of Los Altos.

Charles and I were anxious. How do you read a piece of writing to one of the writers you admire most?

Wilkinson read the beginning of what we had drafted, and I finished it.

Wally sat in his chair with his hands folded. "That's it?" he said. "You came all the way to California to read me that?" He then lit into the Bush policies with such incredulousness that we were shamed for our timidity, which we had seen as progressive and brave.

True eloquence has an edge, sharp and clean.

A month later Stegner was awarded the 1992 National Medal of Arts, but turned it down because he was "troubled" by the political controls placed upon the National Endowment for the Arts and the National Endowment for the Humanities under the tyranny of leadership by administrators like Lynne Cheney.

For Stegner, the integrity of wilderness and the integrity of art were the same thing, something to be honored and protected as a wellspring of inspiration.

Both Robert Mapplethorpe's orchids and the threatened tundra on the Arctic's coastal plain deserved our respect and restraint as harbingers of imagination. Creativity is another form of open space, whose very nature is to disturb, disrupt, and "bring us to tenderness."

When Wally spoke about "the native home of hope," it was in direct response to his belief and imperative that we can "create a society to match the scenery."

I returned to Utah, our home in the desert. My politics would remain local.

After the 1994 Republican sweep in the midterm elections, the Utah congressional delegation, led by Representative Jim Hansen and Senator Orrin Hatch, announced they were going to draft a Utah wilderness bill once and for all. They were tired of the decades-old contention over Utah's wildlands. Hansen and Hatch believed, alongside the "Gingrich revolution," they had the political power to get what they wanted—as little wilderness as possible. The governor, Michael Leavitt, reminded them that by law, they had to conduct public hearings. So in 1995, January through May, local hearings were held throughout the state. More than 70 percent of the people in Utah wanted more wilderness, not less, advocating for the Citizens' Proposal, which at the time protected 5.7 million acres of wilderness. Utahns were told that their voice would not only be heard but respected.

Formal congressional subcommittee hearings were held in Cedar City, Utah.

There were three panels: the political panel, the extractive industry panel, and the conservation panel. I had been asked by the conservation community to speak. We would testify last.

Congressman Jim Hansen and his colleagues sat on a riser above us, designed to intimidate. As I stood to speak, Hansen began shuffling through his papers, yawning, coughing, anything to show his boredom and displeasure. I was halfway through my testimony when it became clear that the congressman wasn't even listening. I stopped mid-sentence. "Congressman Hansen, I have been a resident of Utah all of my life. Is there anything I can say to you that might in some way alter your perspective on wilderness?"

He looked over the top of his glasses perched at the end of his nose, slowly leaned on his elbows, and said simply, "I'm sorry, Ms. Williams, there is something about your voice I cannot hear."

And then it was over.

I don't think he was referring to the quality of the microphone. Congressman Hansen's remarks became a metaphor, a symbolic representation of our delegation's inability—no, refusal—to hear what we were saying about wilderness.

One month later Hansen and Hatch presented the 1995 Utah Public Lands Management Act, proposing protection of only 1.8 million acres out of the 22 million acres administered through the Bureau of Land Management.

It was a slap in the face of democracy, a betrayal of public trust in the name of our public commons. Outraged, I kept thinking, *What can I do as a citizen?*

I wrote an op-ed piece for *The New York Times*, "Open for Business," outlining the grave inadequacies of this bill created by Utah's congressional delegation. The Utah Public Lands Management Act of 1995 undermined the 1964 Wilderness Act by opening up previously protected lands to oil and gas development.

In July, a special hearing was held before the Senate Committee on Energy and Natural Resources in Washington, D.C. Senator Hatch and Senator Bob Bennett both testified on behalf of their bill. Again, there were three panels. Again, the conservation panel was last. And once again, I testified with three other Utahns to support the Citizens' Proposal for 5.7 million acres, part of America's Red Rock Wilderness Act already before Congress, not the Hatch-Bennett bill advocating only 1.8 million acres.

The panel on industry had finished its testimony— given by representatives ranging from the Utah Farm Bureau to the oil and gas companies. The conservation committee was next. Mayor Phillip Bimstein from Springdale, Utah, gateway to Zion National Park, was the first speaker. Two minutes into his allotted five-minute testimony, committee chairman Senator Larry Craig, a Republican from Idaho, stood up and said boisterously, "This one is yours, Senator Hatfield," and then he walked out. Mark Hatfield was a lame duck from Oregon. Phillip had to stop his testimony while this "changing of the gavel" occurred, and after the disruption, Senator Hatfield looked at the small-town mayor and said, "Your time is up— next!"

It was more than rude and ill-mannered, it was disrespectful of the democratic process. For the rest of the hearing Senator Hatfield read a book during our testimonies. Basically, we ended up speaking to the wall. Our consolation: our testimonies were entered into the *Congressional Record*.

We left the nation's capital disheartened and discouraged. It was hard not to ask, "What is the point?"

When I returned home, I met with Stephen Trimble, a fellow writer, for coffee. We talked about the wilderness debate and what was happening in Congress.

"Perhaps Congress can't hear one voice," I said,

"but maybe they can hear a community of voices." We had been talking about creating a small chapbook to celebrate Utah wilderness.

"Perhaps now is the time," Steve said.

We wrote an impassioned letter to our friends. It began: "We need your help." The letter went on to say, "Utah's redrock wilderness is in jeopardy. Here's the political situation we are up against . . . We know you love Utah's wildlands. We are asking you to please write the most eloquent, beautiful essay or poem you have ever written. We cannot pay you, and we need your essay in three weeks." We mailed the letter to twenty-five western writers, each one with firsthand knowledge of America's redrock wilderness.

Miraculously, in three weeks we had twenty original pieces from a community of writers committed to language and landscape, essays as heartfelt as anything we had ever read.

The roster of writers included John McPhee, Barry Lopez, Bill Kittredge, Scott Momaday, Ann Zwinger, Richard Shelton, and U.S. poet laureate Mark Strand, all powerful voices within American letters. Karen Shepherd, a former congresswoman from Utah, contributed. Charles Wilkinson contributed his water law expertise. Mardy Murie, who was turning one hundred that year, allowed us to publish a piece of hers regarding wilderness in general. At the other end of the age spectrum was Rick Bass, thirty-eight at the time, a muscular writer and wilderness advocate from Yaak, Montana. We asked T. H. Watkins, the distinguished historian and lover of Utah, if he would consider writing a foreword, which he did.

We sought a designer, again a friend of ours, Trent Alvey, who graciously agreed to work on the project for free. We received six thousand dollars from a local foundation sponsored by Annette and Ian Cumming, great supporters of conservation efforts in Utah. This paid for the printing costs of a thousand chapbooks.

We organized the essays in a sequence we felt was the most powerful progression of ideas. We had to work quickly. We knew the biographies were important to show the standing of the writers involved. We wanted signatures from each of the writers to add solidarity and depth. There was a flurry and frenzy of writers faxing their signatures to us so we could incorporate them into the design, adding power and presence to the book.

We included a map, with a list of all the proposed wilderness areas within the Citizens' Proposal for America's Red Rock Wilderness. In two weeks we had our book. We called this anthology *Testimony: Writers of the West Speak on Behalf of Utah Wilderness.*

Good work is a stay against despair.

The Southern Utah Wilderness Alliance, a smart

and scrappy grassroots advocacy group, helped us place *Testimony* in the hands of every member of Congress. This is the power of collaboration, of one community supporting and helping another.

In mid-September we held a press conference in Washington, D.C., on the Triangle, next to the U.S. Capitol. The historian Tom Watkins spoke, placing this anthology in a political context alongside Wallace Stegner's *This Is Dinosaur*, a collection of writings to stop the dam on the Green River in Dinosaur National Monument in the 1950s. Congressmen Maurice Hinchey and Bruce Vento, cosponsors of America's Red Rock Wilderness Act, were present. They publicly accepted copies of *Testimony*, acknowledging this chapbook as the equivalent of a literary bill brought to the halls of Congress by American writers. They promised to carry these words to their colleagues. They spoke eloquently about wilderness as a spiritual birthright belonging to all Americans. Senator Russ Feingold was also in attendance, with a vow that he would take *Testimony* to the floor of the Senate and defeat the Utah Public Lands Management Act of 1995.

Following the press conference, a reporter from *The Washington Post* approached Steve and me.

"What a waste of time," he said. "Do you have any idea how much paper gets passed around Congress? You are so naive. This will never see the light of day."

I was incredulous, ready to have a good, spirited debate. Steve had a calmer presence of mind. He said to the reporter, "Writing is always an act of faith."

Copies of *Testimony* were, in fact, passed throughout Congress. I was able to deliver a copy to Mrs. Clinton, who promised to present *Testimony* to the president.

We placed a copy in the hands of Vice President Gore and key members of the Clinton administration.

In March 1996, the Utah Public Lands Management Act of 1995 finally found its way to the Senate floor. The Senate went into a filibuster. What a filibuster needs is words. Senator Bill Bradley of New Jersey rose to his feet. "With all due respect, Senators Hatch and Bennett, these wildlands belong to all Americans, not just those living in Utah. I would like to read from one of my constituents, John McPhee: 'Basin, Range, Basin, Range . . .' And Senator Bradley read John McPhee's essay in its entirety. He was followed by other senators reading from *Testimony*. Throughout the filibuster, essay after essay celebrating sandstone buttes and mesas was read out loud, saturating time and space within the Senate Chamber. The Utah Public Lands Management Act of 1995 died on the Senate floor.

Testimony is now part of the *Congressional Record*.

Six months later, on September 18, 1996, President William Jefferson Clinton designated the new Grand Staircase-Escalante National Monument, protecting nearly two million acres of wilderness in Utah. The environmental community held strong, and the political climate was right in the midst of a presidential election. Afterward, President Clinton held up a copy of *Testimony* and said, "This little book made a difference."

One never knows the tangible effects of literature, but on that particular day, looking north into the vast wildlands of the Colorado Plateau, one could believe in the collective power of a chorus of voices.

Driving back from the ceremony, I felt like a sister to Thelma and Louise, seated in their light blue convertible with the arch of sky above me. Not quite an outlaw and not yet choosing to drive off a cliff, I was still free to move in big, open country that for now remained wild. Democracy demands we speak and act outrageously. We can change the world if our view is long and focused with friends drawn lovingly around the place we call home.

More than a decade later America's Red Rock Wilderness Act continues to be a bill before Congress, now advocating for 9.2 million acres of protected wilderness in Utah. Our voices are still singing on the margins.

XLI

I AM IN JAIL because I was speeding, driving under a suspended license.

I am in jail because I didn't have the money to pay the fine.

I am in jail because one night can't be that bad.

I am in jail because part of me thinks I deserve to be.

INSIDE

Three sets of doors open and close behind me, then lock shut. I enter the women's pod, where twelve prisoners like myself are dressed in orange. It is a crowded room, with seven metal bunk beds; a toilet, sink, and shower; and four bolted-down tables with attached chairs that swing out from under them. The walls are cinder blocks painted white, with no windows, only fluorescent lights. The floor is covered with shiny linoleum squares.

The women are young. I am the oldest by decades. They are pale and puffy. Some are sleeping. Some are lying on their bunks, facing the wall in a fetal position. Some are brushing their hair. Some are smoking tampons, imagining them as cigarettes. Nobody says anything, and neither do I.

A deputy walks me to my bunk, and I am instructed to put my plastic bin under it. The bin contains utensils, a plastic cup, a comb, a pair of orange socks, a toothbrush, toothpaste, four sheets of lined paper, and a thin plastic cylinder of blue ink, the kind inside a Bic pen.

One by one I hear the women's sentences: forgery, child abuse, making meth and selling it, fraud.

I understand the sentence about fraud. I am a writer about place who is never home. It's about time, time to take an honest look: Selfish. Self-absorbed. Overweight. Overwrought. Neither Brooke nor I had two thousand dollars to pay my fine. In debt. In denial. Time to see my relationship with my family for what it is—broken. Time to recognize my addiction to a lifestyle that is not sustainable. How many times have I told myself it is time to change my life?

What is the sound of a woman's voice in prison? "Fuck this . . . fuck that . . . fuck them." Two women talk about how there's nothing uglier than women who cuss.

"*Fuck* is such an ugly word. We need to clean up our language. We'd feel better about ourselves." They turn around and look at me.

"I say it all the time."

"You don't seem the type."

"I am the type."

I am a woman doing time with other women doing time at the Caribou County Jail in Idaho. Dressed in orange on the inside, we all appear the same. Anyone can fall through the cracks of justice. No one is immune. But I also know—even as I will be shackled with chains around my wrists, waist, and ankles when taken to my court hearing tomorrow—I will be free to leave after a court date is set. My time in jail, not for a noble cause, is a day, a night, and a day. Most of these women will stay for weeks, months, years, with the knowledge that once in the system, it's tough to get out. Nothing is fair, be it birth or luck or fate.

At night, when most of the women are asleep, I hear the cries of a mother who gave birth in prison and was never allowed to hold her son before they took him away. She holds her index finger several times a day, imagining her baby's grip while nursing.

"It's okay to cry," a woman whispers to her. "I wish I could."

Clipped wings. Caged birds. The only freedom here is the freedom to tell the truth. There is little judgment because the judgments have been made. It's the judgments on the outside that have put us on the inside. And so we share our stories, true or false. Who cares?

All we have is time.

The sentence of waiting is what we've been given. Five squares of light have appeared on the white wall across from where I am sitting. Now the squares are ascending like a ladder toward the ceiling. I wonder if this is how dreams of escape begin.

OUTSIDE

Brooke is waiting for me outside, wearing an orange T-shirt in solidarity. He hugs me. I dissolve. Driving home, we pass Freedom, Wyoming. I stare out the window at the autumn leaves. "Why do I hate the color orange when my favorite colors are red and yellow?" one of the women asked me inside. I had no answer.

XLII

CAN YOU BE INSIDE AND OUTSIDE at the same time?

I think this is where I live.

I think this is where most women live.

———

I know this is where writers live.

Inside to write. Outside to glean.

I want to revisit the book of Ruth. Ruth, the Moabite, who has lost her husband to death, chooses to leave her place of origin and accompany her widowed mother-in-law, Naomi, an Israelite, back to her homeland in Bethlehem.

"For wherever you go, I will go," Ruth says. "And wherever you lodge, I will lodge; Your people shall be my people, and your God, my God. Where you die, I will die; and there will I be buried . . ."

Ruth's voice and vow embodies faithful love in action, what the Hebrew word *hesed* celebrates as loving-kindness, a central virtue within the Jewish faith. Now in Israel, Ruth, as an outsider, says to Naomi, "Let me go to the fields and pick up the left-over grain behind anyone in whose eyes I find favor."

Ruth becomes a gleaner, finding in the furrows what remains from the harvest of barley to nourish the two women. The owner of the fields, whose name is Boaz, is a relative of Naomi's. He notices the humble beauty of Ruth and instructs the reapers to leave more grain for her to gather. In time, they meet; they marry. Ruth gives birth to a baby boy named Obed, whom both women mother. Obed becomes the grandfather of King David of Israel.

The book of Ruth honors the loyal bonds between women. To care for one another reaps the harvest of love. Ruth's empathy and toil gives birth to authentic power. An outsider who brings compassion to her bereaved mother-in-law becomes the ancestress of Israel's most benevolent king, who becomes an ancestor to the Divine Child and Savior Jesus Christ.

What do we glean from the stories of other women?

What am I gleaning in the furrows of my mother's journals?

I forage for the details left, overlooked, discarded. I will use everything in this story she has given me before her death and afterward to find out what is there and what is not there, and then begin culling the grain from the chaff, savoring what is essential.

Mother gave me my voice by withholding hers, both in life and in death. Her creativity presided in her home. She spoke through gestures, largely quiet and graceful. A letter. A meal. A walk together. Her touch. She lived on a private, elegant plain.

Mimi gave me my voice by proclaiming hers: directly, honestly, and, at times, shockingly. When Brooke and I went to tell her we were getting married, she said, "How wonderful! And if it doesn't work out, you can always get a divorce."

But I believe my own voice continues to be found wherever I am being present and responding from my heart, moment by moment. My voice is born repeatedly in the fields of uncertainty.

XLIII

Love is where I both find my voice and lose it. I can touch the place in me where I vanished in the hands of a lover, crazy and foolish, driven and mad. I became a wild boar rooting in disturbed soil for truffles.

And they were truffles, wonderful and rich, but occasional.

In love, the tongue writes wet words on the skin in a shining script where letters disappear like invisible ink, leaving only sensation.

The most beautiful words cannot be written, un-fortunately. Fortunately. We would have to be able to write with our eyes, with wild eyes, with the tears of our eyes, with the frenzy of a gaze, with the skin of our hands.

And so . . .

In love, I whisper.
In love, I cry.
In love, I cry out.
In love, I breathe—we breathe together.
We hold the silence, suspended.

The days when love was for me a matter of art.

But in love, I also lash out, speak the unspeakable, and attempt murder with my mouth. In these moments I am beyond rage, I ravage the one before me in an act of revenge. Love is a humiliation. I retaliate. If you cannot be intimate, then I will make you run for your life. I want you. I want you gone. I want you here. I want you very far away.

This is how I want you: larger and smaller stronger and weaker taller and trembling more, more out of breath than I more burning more penetrating bolder bossier more yielding more frightened narrower and more relentless than you are more than I.

Desire speaks through the body. His eyes locked on mine as we made love on a day into night until dawn, when the humidity was high and the only sounds were the sustained sighs that break into cries with skin sliding back and forth with the sweat of sweet friction and elegant finesse.

It is "the lover's discourse." *What I hide by my language, my body utters.* The necessity. The connivance. Only us. The incalculable two. Understanding love as madness. What can be done? We are done. Never.

Everything she never would have said (precisely because of her concern with respecting accepted limits, and not offending good taste), love said it— immodestly, immediately, inconsiderably, in . . . Love said: ". . . . . . ."

And yet he stayed at the entrance.
Because in love all is not love.
Because in love not all is love.

To my mentor in words, Hélène Cixous, her words are my words are my confession to say, "Thank you, yes, exactly."

"You corrupted me," he said.
"We corrupted each other," she said.

Our drama is that we live in a state of mutual invasion.

But I am just a woman who thinks her duty is not to forget.

I come from a woman.

Women are not to be satisfied.

And I? I drink, I burn, I gather dreams.
And sometimes, I tell a story.

XLIV

My MOTHER'S JOURNALS are a love story. Love and power. What she gave and what she withheld were hers to choose. Love is power. Power is not love. Both can be brutal. Both dance with control. Both can be intoxicating, leaving us out of control. But in the end it is love, not power, that endures and shows us the consequences of our choices. My mother chose me as the recipient of her pages, empty pages.

She left me her "Cartographies of Silence." I will never know her story. I will never know what she was trying to tell me by telling me nothing.

But I can imagine.

And isn't this the beautiful truth of love and power?

"Most of my injuries come from the stereotype." These are not my words. I plagiarize. I will not tell you who wrote them. Instead, I will claim them as my own because I have so thoroughly inhabited them; they could be written by no one else but me.

We borrow. We steal. We purchase what we need and buy what we don't. We acquire things, people, places, all in the process of losing ourselves. Busyness is the religion of distraction. I cannot talk to you, because I have too much to do.

I cannot do what I want, because I am doing what I must. Must I forever walk away from what is real and true and hard?

When it comes to words, rather than using our own voice, authentic and unpracticed, we steal someone else's to shield our fear. And in my mother's case, she let me fill in the blanks. This is my inheritance.

I am my mother, but I'm not.

I am my grandmother, but I'm not.

I am my great-grandmother, but I'm not.

Patterned behavior alternates like shadow and light. Pain in love is a pattern that repeats itself until we recognize it as destructive. *"No one lives in this room without living through some kind of crisis. No one lives in this room without confronting the whiteness of the wall."* We can change, evolve, and transform our own conditioning. We can choose to move like water rather than be molded like clay. Life spirals in and then spirals out on any given day. It does not have to be one way, one truth, one voice. Nor does love have to be all or nothing. Neither does power. What is positive and what is negative is not absolute.

"Let it go—" Mother would say whenever I asked her what I should keep or give away. Her answer was always the same.

Empty pages become possibilities.

XLV

To look at the script of Nushu is to see bird tracks, crows walking deliberately down a narrow path of snow. It is a linear and elegant calligraphy, very different from the boxed characters of traditional Chinese. This is the secret script of women, used for hundreds of years in the rural villages of Jiangyong in Hunan Province of China.

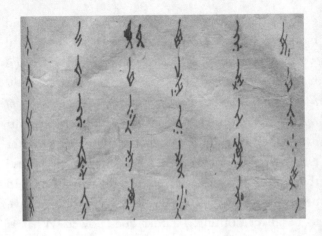

This ancient script has a genealogy that may predate the oracle bone etchings of the Shang Dynasty, 1600–1100 B.C., identified as belonging to a women's society that worshipped birds. The symbol for a bird's head is the character for a woman's head. Women and birds were interchangeable, shape-shifting inscriptions carved on bones and the carapaces of turtles, an archetype for the Earth Goddess, who presides over fertility, continuity, and wisdom.

Nushu is seeded in the language of illiterate women, women who were not allowed to go to school as late as the twentieth century. These whispered writings were passed on from mother to daughter and the closest of friends, "sworn sisters," carefully guarded, written on the folds of paper fans, embroidered on handkerchiefs or written discreetly inside the slippers that bound their feet.

One of the last Nushu practitioners, Yang Huanyi, was born in 1909. She explained how Nushu was a way women could speak to themselves outside of the language of men. Women in the village would make hand-bound books written in Nushu and pass them from one woman to the next as gifts. They were largely autobiographical. Sometimes, simple; other times, profound. When the woman who wrote them died, the women closest to her would burn them as an offering to accompany her in the afterlife, a conjoining of word and spirit.

Beside a well, one won't thirst; beside a sister, one won't despair.

Special books known as "sanzhaoshu" or "three-day missives" were also written in Nushu by a mother to her daughter on the occasion of her wedding. Here, mothers celebrated the union of the newly married couple, lovingly, yet at the same time grieved the separation from their daughter. Other women in the bride's life added their wisdom to this wedding keepsake. Empty pages were reserved for the bride's own musings in her personalized script. The book became an honored and precious testament, another secret text written in code, between the Jiangyong women.

My Mother's Journals are written in code.

Nushu was rediscovered in 1981 by outside linguistic scholars. Cathy Silber asks of women's scripts, in general, "Who writes, who writes what, who reads it, who cares?"

The Japanese suppressed Nushu during their rule of China in the 1940s, fearing it could be used as a cipher against them. The Red Guards had similar concerns during the Cultural Revolution.

Today, original texts written in Nushu are extremely rare, having been burned or lost or sold. Yang Huanyi died on September 20, 2004, and the living context for the fifteen hundred Nushu characters vanished with her.

Women have always written in code as a way to protect themselves. Nushu was a "proper female activity," a script that became threatening only when the inner chambers of thought crossed over into the outer chambers of action. Hélène Cixous writes, "We must learn to speak the language women speak when there is no one there to correct us."

XLVI

June 1, 1975
Dearest Terry,

Tomorrow will begin the first day of your life with Brooke. Always keep it exciting and vital and interesting. A woman can really be the electrifying force in a marriage, but it takes a lot of unselfish loving. I do believe that God intended that a woman be made of qualities to give and give and give, and only when we give to the man we love are we really glorified.

Men are so vulnerable and it is up to a wife to keep her "nest" peaceful, beautiful and in harmony with life; removed from the turmoil of the world.

I pray that your relationship with Brooke will always be a challenge to you. Remember that you compliment each other not consume each other.

Thank you, Terry, for creating such a loving atmosphere in our home. I feel so blessed to have the opportunity to be your Mother. It has been such a beautiful relationship; first as a mother and daughter, as dearest friends, and now as two women very much in love with their husbands. You have given

my life dimensions beyond descriptions. My deepest
wish for you is to have a son or daughter of your own
and experience the joy that comes from complete
sharing as we have.

I really don't feel you are leaving this home, I feel
blessed that we are bringing another beautiful person
into it.

Please take with you tomorrow to the Temple this
gift and know that as you hold it, so do you hold the
love of all of your family. We all love you so much.

May this very sacred day be one of eternal
blessing to you and Brooke.

Mother

On the outside of the envelope she wrote, "To My
Special Daughter, With My Love."

Inside the envelope was a white handkerchief
embroidered with lace.

My Mother's Journals are a collection of white
handkerchiefs.

Brooke and I have been married for almost four
decades. A marriage is among the most private of
landscapes. It is also the most demanding if both part-
ners are to maintain their individuality and equipoise.
How do you contain within a domestic arrangement a
howling respect for the wild in each other?

"Always keep it exciting and vital and interesting . . ." Mother issued a challenge without instructions.

In watching my parents' marriage, I came to believe their strength was in the time they spent together: taking trips, long and short, weekends out, the conversation they shared while driving big distances in the West. They had their own lives outside of their children. And we knew it.

In Brooke's and my marriage, I believe our strength is in the time we spend apart.

Rilke provided us with a map: "Love consists in this, that two solitudes protect and touch and greet each other." I need my solitude. Brooke needs his freedom. When we come together, we meet whole.

But sometimes the distances become too great, and words don't help in the articulation of our souls when we want to share where we've been and who we have become.

I have never been as lonely as I have been in my marriage. I have also never been more seen or more protected. Love has little to do with it. Marriage is more sandstone than granite, similar to the terrain of southern Utah: the geography of mountains, canyons, and plateaus. The weathering creates the redrock windows and bridges. Beauty is transformed over time, and not without destruction.

Landscape is dynamic. So is marriage. Brooke and I have changed, and changed each other. What has been washed and eroded away is as important as what remains.

What remains for Brooke and me is conversation, our shared love of ideas. We have never stopped loving all things wild and unruly, including each other. We raised each other, grew up together. And as a couple, we have given birth to each other, both as lovers and refugees in a culture foreign to our true nature. The feral fury of our twenties is such a different fire in our fifties. Deeper, fuller, the fire fanned now is just as intense and surprising because of the spaces we honor between us that hold a history. Brooke remains a mystery.

Big Sur is a place we return to for renewal, a ragged edge for condors, crashing waves, and hot springs. On one particular day it was raining. We were staying in a small guest cottage of friends. We lit candles, made tea, and read—the kind of day you dream about, cozy and calm. But after dinner we became restless. Brooke suggested an art project.

"Let's cut up magazines."

I burst out laughing.

"No, I'm serious," he said. "We can make a collage of who we are at this moment in time."

I was skeptical, which amused Brooke.

"Don't think about it," he said. "Just cut and paste." He dismantled a cardboard box we had in the car for transporting food. He cut it in two. "Here."

We had brought enough magazines between us for catch-up reading to supply us with material. And so we staked out our own territory on the floor and began cutting up *Oprah*, *Orion*, *Vanity Fair*, *People*, and past issues of *The New Yorker*. A few copies of *National Geographic* were in the cottage, and we took the liberty of poaching from them as well.

Brooke poured us each a glass of wine. I replaced the candles that had burned down during the day and lit them. Among flickering shadows and the sound of rain we went to work.

During the two hours we were making our visual narratives, I would look over at Brooke, intense in his creation, and he would catch my eye as I was laying down a particular phrase, neither one of us speaking. And then we were done.

We both visited each other's collage, a stratigraphy of the self through image and words. Each of us told our story to the other. I had no idea where Brooke had been living internally, but the figure painted in mud with hands on fire and feet made of roots told me everything I needed to know. I particularly loved the Raven's head.

Jade Cove. Sand Dollar Beach. Big Sur. It is six months after the fires. Nature has a voice and it is often brutal without cause. Waves break and sea foam gathers around my ankles. There is a continuum here on the edge of America that I seek.

Wave after wave rolls in aquamarine translucent waters touching sands from the long reach of Asia.

East. West.

Brooke is walking the beach with his sweater over one shoulder coming toward me. If I was to write the story of our marriage, I would write it on these sands where nothing is permanent, just as I write with water on paper, my book of waves.

Tidal—this is the nature of our partnership—high tide, low tide—minus and full, always tied to the Moon. Here, Now. Just this morning, we awoke to its light, yellow-orange, floating above the horizon as a cradle, a boat.

We rose and walked outside the cottage perched above the folding cliffs and watched the Moon disappear at dawn.

The hand is a wave upon the body called a caress.

Making love is making waves—one after the other—carrying us deeper into the flood of forgetting and remembering, retreating and returning to why we are alive.

He who knows that this body is the foam of a wave . . . goes on and follows his path.

—The Dhammapada

My path is the embodiment of waves.

My marriage is the stone I carry in my pocket as a secret, a source of grounding, a mystery I turn in hand.

If my marriage is a secret, it is also large enough to hold secrets that I have learned not to tell. This is the nature of intimacy; discretion.

Later Brooke and I argue over whether or not the white long-legged birds roosting on the rocks are great white egrets or cattle egrets. Brooke says cattle. I say great. I know I am right. He thinks he is. We will consult *Peterson's Field Guide to Western Birds* when we return to the cottage. This is after all, the book that brought us together.

XLVII

WHEN I WANT to see the furthest into my soul, I will write a sentence by hand and then write another sentence over it, followed by another. An entire paragraph will live in one line, and no one else can read it. That is the point. On occasions, in a café, I can fill an entire paper place mat on both sides. On a plane, the paper bag for airsickness is my canvas. Anything will do: the backs of business cards, receipts, napkins, any scrap of paper. A friend of mine calls it my disease. I call it my confessional.

It looks like this:

My name for this kind of writing is *repetations*. I am not alone. Robert Walser, the German modernist from the beginning of the twentieth century, wrote in "microscripts." They were almost impossible to decipher. He wrote in "a tiny pencil script" described as between one to two millimeters in height. One block of Walser's text that was two inches tall and two and three-quarters inches wide held 113 words. Through the minuscule movements of his pencil, he was liberated from the elegance and eloquence of his former pen.

Susan Bernofsky called his penmanship "obsessive rows crawling across page after tiny page like columns of ants . . . resembling nothing so much as a blurry or distant view of the newly and monotonously printed columns of text on a newspaper page."

Walser's writings have been called "an aesthetics of bewilderment." His intention was not to keep secrets, but to represent a diminutive *Kurrent* script, with medieval roots, fashionable in German-speaking countries during his time.

Deemed schizophrenic, Robert Walser was admitted to the Waldau Sanitarium in 1929. His writing was used as a diagnostic symptom, one of many that kept him institutionalized until his death. I wonder if his micrography was more than a physical manifestation of illness—instead, an aesthetic choice that allowed him to experiment, another way for him to read not just his mind but his soul.

"May my words be dipped one by one in a bath of deliberation until the language flowing from my pen abounds with a black velvet profundity. Not a syllable will be a fib . . ."

One microscript was titled "A Will to Shake That Refined Individual." If we adopt a personalized script, even a secret one, we are released from the need to perfect content. We are freed from our public morality. We can set an honest path of inquiry with our pen, or in the case of Walser, his pencil.

"This pencil method," he writes, "has great meaning for me. The writer of these lines experienced a time when he hideously, frightfully hated his pen, I can't begin to tell you how sick of it he was; he became an outright idiot the moment he made the least use of it; and to free himself from this pen malaise he began to pencil-sketch, to scribble, fiddle about. With the aid of my pencil I was better able to play, to write . . ."

My own hand, with pen in place, bushwhacks through my psyche, cutting through the dense understory of random thoughts. As my black pen circles back on itself, destroying as it creates, hiding what has just been written as another sentence walks across the newly exposed words, I am freed. My repetitions tell me the truth the moment they are drawn. And then, in the process of layered language, a path is cleared. I see where I need to go. These ephemeral paragraphs, which even I cannot decode once they have been tracked, turn into reimagined glyphs. Their meaning resides in the process of obfuscation. There is an art to writing, and it is not always disclosure. The act itself can be beautiful, revelatory, and private.

"A will to shake that refined individual, to rattle him about as if he were a scraggly tree bearing only isolated jittery leaves, seems to be stirring within me."

It is precisely these jitters that set me on this course of cryptic calligraphy. I often tear my repetitions into shreds, creating paper shards to scatter in the garden. If only my mother had known I was her sister instead of her daughter.

XLVIII

THE DOOR WAS OPEN. I let my eyes adjust. Inside, the Virgin was receiving the news of her miraculous conception. Her hand was protecting her heart. The archangel Gabriel knelt before her with the gift of a lily. A bouquet of pink roses from the garden adorned the altar. I sat on a wooden pew for a long time. There were no people present, only those painted by Ghirlandaio in this small Italian church on the road to Donnini, where Dante was said to have visited.

I knelt at the confessional. No one was behind the velvet red curtain or between the perforated wall, but I wanted to feel this posture. Something new. My body settled into my knees. I leaned my cheek against where the ear of the priest would be.

"Why would I tell you anything?" I whispered.

It was not what I had intended to say. Leaving one orthodoxy means leaving all orthodoxies. I got up slowly, out of practice from kneeling on such a hard surface, and walked to the altar, where Mary was meeting the Angel's gaze. I lit a tall, thin taper and placed it in a cast-iron clip molded in the shape of a scallop. The Virgin glowed. The gold pattern on her gown was meant to illuminate light, not to impress. The church became darker as the flame intensified. I stared at the flame. I closed my eyes, but the flame remained, still and numinous, and I recalled a poet's line after just such a gesture: "Now, you have seen eternity."

XLIX

IT FELT LIKE AN ANNUNCIATION. It wasn't a decision. Call it an initiation to what I feared most: a loss of self through love—naively, willingly, obsessively. It has been my spiritual annihilation through fate. And it has been physical.

At fifty, I said yes, with my husband, Brooke, to Louis Gakumba. We created a home and a family for him in America while he received his college education. He was twenty-four years old, the son of a Congolese prince. He had been my translator in Rwanda. Some things cannot be translated.

Everything about my relationship with Louis has surprised me.

Here is what I will tell you:

Roland Barthes says, "That which cannot be named is a disturbance."

"It is not possible to satisfy women," a friend said. "We are disturbed if we have children too young. Disturbed if we have them later. Disturbed if we don't have children at all."

I am not Louis's mother, but I have become a mother, which is an unspoken agreement to be forever vulnerable. Unbidden, my eyes slide to the clock day and night and I wonder where he is, if he is safe, on the road or at home, if he has had enough to eat, if he is healthy, if he needs anything from me. It doesn't matter the age of our relations, conventional or unorthodox, we suffer and learn by heart.

There is a common phrase in Rwanda, "He has a good heart." How does one know? We know the quality of another's heart through her voice. Not the sound, although it is a cue. Not through words, although they present an idea. I most often feel the tenor of another's heart through tone and the feeling that enters my body when they speak.

"Once you know that you have a voice," Louis said, "it's no longer the voice that matters, but what is behind the voice."

Louis has improved the quality of my listening.

In Rwanda, they say a person's silence can be heard as a lion's roar.

L

WE WERE IN MEXICO. Brooke was inside the casita, reading. I floated on my back in the pool outside, where grackles bathed. I watched clouds. Louis was watching me. He stepped into the cold pool. He was interested in learning how to float.

"An act of faith," I said. And continued floating on my back, my arms outstretched like a cross, buoyant in the water. I stood up; the water rippled out from my waist. "All you have to do is relax, lean back, and look up at the sky." He leaned back as my hands slipped under him, supporting his spine, and he floated. For a blessed moment, he floated. Then, his body tensed. He swallowed some water, he coughed, he jerked, and he quickly collapsed into himself and stood upright. Shaking uncontrollably, he got out of the pool and went inside.

Louis said, "Let's not talk about it."

I said, "You are trying to silence me."

He said, "I have told you too much. It is better to

stay quiet. I am forcing myself to go back to who I used to be."

"You cannot go back." I paused. "Words have a way—" and then I stopped.

"A way of what?" he asked.

And I disappeared, watching the shadows of palms swaying, quivering on the white stucco walls of the villa we inhabited.

"Your voice is the wildest thing you own," Brooke says to me. "And you're giving it away. You can't see it. Your obsession is blinding you." He is angry. He is talking in shorthand. "You're losing yourself."

It's after midnight. Louis and I had been talking on the porch. Walking back to Brooke and our casita, I see a beam of light on the beach. Brooke's headlamp. He is on his knees, building a sculpture out of the plastic he's been collecting on the beach. It's a sand castle of sorts, more Gaudí than Disney, with a pink flip-flop as a drawbridge and a doll's arm as a turret. Colored bottle caps are pressed into the sand walls, creating a mosaic. Toothbrushes become raised flags. He is silent. He has said all he's going to say.

The waves come up and flood the castle and retreat as quickly. Brooke is undeterred. He keeps building.

I am standing on the sand, the surf rushing

around my ankles. I have been here before. Where I haven't been is what I have experienced with Louis, feeling responsible for a life, yet a life that is already powerfully formed. I focus completely on what has my attention. Louis has had my attention. I wrap my arms around myself, shaking.

"Thank you," I say.

Brooke looks at me. I am indeed blinded. He turns off his headlamp. Kneeling down on the sand, I join him as we begin repairing what has been eroded.

It is the winter solstice. It is also a lunar eclipse. Brooke and I stand with Louis on the edge of the jungle, which is sizzling with insects, and witness the Sun devouring the Moon. In time the Moon becomes an overripened peach suspended in the sky. The shadow inches away just as it had come, and we watch the Moon reclaim its full illumination.

If you clap your hands before the Temple of the Sun in Chichén Itzá, the voice of the quetzal calls back to you. It is more than an echo. The Maya built an architecture of belief. The presence of the quetzal, sacred bird of the gods, has never left. It knows to withhold its voice until summoned.

Destroy your stray sentences. It is not safe to do otherwise.

I told my husband life is an act of faith. He said no, it is a choice.

My Mother's Journals are an act of faith and a choice.

LI

"How is your shadow—your honorable shadow?" This was a customary greeting between friends in Japan, a recognition that what we reject is as important as what we embrace.

I walk with my shadow behind me, sometimes ahead, and often to the side. It is my capricious companion: visible, then hidden, amorphous. A shadow is never created in darkness. It is born of light. We can be blind to it and blinded by it. Our shadow asks us to look at what we don't want to see. If we refuse to face our shadow, it will project itself on someone else so we have no choice but to engage.

My Mother's Journals are a projection screen.

My Mother's Journals are a blinding light.

My Mother's Journals are a glaring truth.

My Mother's Journals are bleached.

My Mother's Journals are sanitized.

My Mother's Journals are clean.

My Mother's Journals are clean sheets.

My Mother's Journals are white flags of surrender.

My Mother's Journals see ghosts.

My Mother's Journals hear voices.

My Mother's Journals smell desire.

My Mother's Journals touch eternity.

My Mother's Journals are a charity.

My Mother's Journals are a cruelty.

My Mother's Journals are a paper cut.

My Mother's Journals are salt.

*My Mother's Journals are made of gauze to wrap
a wound.*

My Mother's Journals are a scrim.

My Mother's Journals are a stage.

My Mother's Journals are scenes painted white.

My Mother's Journals are programs never printed.

My Mother's Journals are reviews never written.

My Mother's Journals are a writer's block.

My Mother's Journals are a writer's conceit.

My Mother's Journals are her vanities revealed.

*My Mother's Journals are her colored hair left
white.*

*My Mother's Journals are the swirls of cold cream
she rubbed on her cheeks.*

My Mother's Journals are her teeth, called veneers.

My Mother's Journals are sun-blocked protection.

My Mother's Journals are the scent of gardenias.

My Mother's Journals are words wafting above the page.

My Mother's Journals are clouds.

My Mother's Journals are bones.

My Mother's Journals have been stolen.

My Mother's Journals are the Elysian Marbles.

My Mother's Journals are Michelangelo's David.

My Mother's Journals are Gertrude Stein's rose.

My Mother's Journals are the tennis matches she won.

My Mother's Journals are the cue ball in a game of pool.

My Mother's Journals are a white tablecloth not yet set.

My Mother's Journals are a white blouse not yet worn.

My Mother's Journals are diapers washed and folded.

My Mother's Journals are T-shirts washed and pressed.

My Mother's Journals are the letters never written.

My Mother's Journals are her "Treasures of Truth."

My Mother's Journals are her scrapbook of tears.

My Mother's Journals are ice, dry ice.

My Mother's Journals are a hoax.

My Mother's Journals are a tease.

My Mother's Journals are a puzzle.

My Mother's Journals tell me nothing.

My Mother's Journals tell me everything.

My Mother's Journals are a tattarrattat.

*My Mother's Journals are a palindrome, to be read
in either direction.*

Backward and forward: I have a friend who was
once my sister. Now we hardly speak, but she often
appears in my dreams. I think of her. The other day
I found a beautiful letter she wrote. I miss her. Ter-
ribly. We were undone by a death; our relationship
was its casualty. In deep pain, we killed each other
with judgments so no memory of closeness would
remain, and now I mourn another death, the death
of a friendship, another loss, another wound, unspoken.

The sin we commit against each other as women
is lack of support. We hurt. We hurt each other. We
hide. We project. We become mute or duplicitous,
and we fester like boiling water until one day we
erupt like a geyser. Do we forget we unravel in grief?
So much can come between us, especially in silence.
The simplest of misunderstandings becomes a jeal-
ousy over time. I have found what I need most to heal
a broken bond is time together—the very thing I
avoid is the thing most desired.

Unexpressed emotion will be expressed somewhere,
somehow, inside or out, most cruelly as unconscious

aggression delivered with a smile or a poisonous cup of tea.

"It is not the sin that carries the shadow but the intent . . . the intent or drive or motive behind the acts we commit," writes Esther Harding in her essay "The Shadow," published in 1941.

The sin I have committed is the sin of adoption. I have adopted a different set of beliefs from the beliefs I was raised to obey. But this definition of sin over time has become my joy. I do have other gods before me, many, and none are a white elderly man sitting on a gilded throne in heaven. Pronghorn antelope holds authority for me, like a priest. Hermit thrush sings with the voice of an angel.

My betrayals have been many, accidental and deliberate, sins of omission and commission. My pen can wound. My words can burn. I know how to disappear. But redemption is always possible. I pray. I repent. I forgive. I am forgiven. I keep a journal to converse with my shadow. And I believe in the power of a loving community to render miracles.

What was my mother's sin? (I do hate this word. Is this Shadow speaking?)

My mother's sin was her secret. Perhaps she had many, three shelves full. Her secrets are well kept through her runic diaries void of words.

The Maya made certain you could stand in the

center of the ball court and speak your secret and the only one who would hear it was the one intended to receive it. This was a construction of truth, not a corruption of sound.

Not everything is meant for all to hear.

Who can judge the intention of another?

What was the intention of my mother's journals?

My Mother's Journals ask me to turn the page.

Again, I recall the mothers I met in prison who mouthed the lyrics of lullabies each night before bed, gripping their own fingers, imagining their babies, the babies they gave birth to but never held, now adopted.

My Mother's Journals have been adopted by me.

One need not write in order to have a voice. A mother speaks to her children through the generations.

LII

SHADOW AND LIGHT are the children who bring us to our knees. Even so, prayers can be short. There are times when what is called for is a song. We rise. With our fingers curled and our hands gripped together, we reach for the soprano's highest notes. The register we achieve can shatter glass. Often moving and more often absurd, this is not theater, but opera.

My Mother's Journals are an opera.

Age has given me arias. Opera is perspective, singing points of view. It amuses me. Opera in the absurd is excessive, chaotic with gilded clichés, where nothing is out of bounds. No gesture is too large, no circumstance too small to be sung over. Hysteria is within the human range of appropriate response. I am amused by opera because it makes my life seem calm by comparison. And opera is all about comparison.

The characters who inhabit opera love who is forbidden, murder who is good, and forgive who has wronged them. They transgress. They transmit their motives through plot and performance. And we are caught in the intricate web of a story spun through the magic of music married to libretto.

And when opera succeeds in reaching its highest calling, which is to move us, I know of no art form that can seize my heart so forcefully. On a winter afternoon in Hanover, New Hampshire, I sat with strangers in a full house watching *Der Rosenkavalier*, Richard Strauss's comic opera of errors. I found myself sobbing as the beautiful, aging Marschallin mused on the passage of time to her young lover, Octavian. I was not alone. Kleenexes were being passed discreetly.

"Opera has the power to warn you that you have wasted your life," writes Wayne Koestenbaum. "You haven't acted on your desires. You've suffered a stunted, vicarious existence. You've silenced your passions. The volume, height, depth, lushness, and excess of operatic utterance reveal, by contrast, how small your gestures have been until now, how impoverished your physicality; you have only used a fraction of your bodily endowment, and your throat is closed."

What other domain in the arts could authenticate and master a word like *falsetto*? "The place where voice goes wrong . . . a useful pleasure with a bad reputation . . . the illusion of truth," Koestenbaum says. He admires it as a "vocal masquerade."

My Mother's Journals are a falsetto, a vocal masquerade.

Opera is an artifice.

My Mother's Journals are an artifice.

Opera demands we pay attention to the spectacle before us, "a grand arena of irreconcilables: music and text, grandeur and tackiness, the aerial and the carnal, the aural and the visible, the modish and the outdated, the living and the dead," Tony Kushner says. "Opera ought to have died out . . ."

But it hasn't.

My father accompanied me to Zurich, where we saw Richard Strauss's *Die Frau ohne Schatten*, known as "the Mount Everest of operas." He said, "I can endure anything for four hours if it has a halftime." There were two intermissions between the three acts.

The Woman Without a Shadow is a fairy tale, a singing archetype, written by the poet Hugo von Hofmannsthal. Consider it variations of a woman's voice.

Here is the story. There are two women: one without a shadow, who lives in the Realm of the Spirits; and one with a shadow, who lives in the Realm of Humans. One is an empress married to an emperor; the other, a wife married to a man who dyes cloth.

The Empress has conceived no child and casts no

shadow. If she cannot find a shadow within three days, her husband will be turned to stone. Red Falcon, the same falcon who struck her down when she was a gazelle (she was capable of shape-shifting in the forest), delivers this curse to the Empress while the Emperor is hunting. Captured by her beauty and fearful he will lose her, the Emperor keeps her in a locked cage.

The Empress is served by a Nurse, and together they descend to Earth to find her a shadow. Disguised as humble servants, they visit the Dyer's Wife, who is unhappy with her husband, bored and unsatisfied by his sexual advances, which are never for pleasure but only for the hope of progeny. The Nurse seduces the Dyer's Wife into a bargain: if she will renounce her future of motherhood and give up her shadow, she will be promised a life of riches and erotic adventures.

On the second day, the Nurse reappears to the Dyer's Wife, with the Empress as witness. She conjures up visions of wealth and a ghostly lover in exchange for the wife's shadow. The Dyer's Wife embraces the lustful apparition, believing this is her path to prosperity and happiness. She is tired of her dull husband and pale life.

Meanwhile, the Emperor follows the Red Falcon into the forest, leading him to the pavilion where his wife and the Nurse are staying. He spies on them. The Emperor can smell the scent of humans on the

Empress. Intermingling of gods and humans is forbidden. He becomes enraged and wants to kill her, but he cannot bring himself to harm the woman he loves.

Back on Earth, the Nurse gives the Dyer a sleeping potion. While he is asleep, she makes her final plea and last glittering offer of a life of pleasure to the Dyer's Wife in exchange for her shadow. Time is running out for the Empress.

Conflicted by her choice, the Dyer's Wife refuses. Guilt ridden by her fantasies, she wakes the Dyer to tell him what she almost traded away for a life of lust and luxury. Moved by his wife's admission, the Dyer wishes to make love to her, but her disgust returns as she realizes that her husband still desires her only for future children.

That night in the forest pavilion, the Empress is tortured by her own guilt about the goodness of the Dyer and the Dyer's Wife, about forcing them into this place of confusion and contempt. She has grown fond of the human couple as she sees their struggle. She cannot take the Dyer's Wife's shadow. She accepts that her husband, the Emperor, will turn to stone.

On the third day, the Dyer's Wife lies to her husband and tells him she has committed adultery. She denounces her future children, the very thing she knows he desires most, and tells the Dyer that she has sold her shadow for pleasure.

The Nurse has succeeded. The Empress will have her shadow and the Emperor will be saved. But the Empress watches the drama. She sees their suffering. The Dyer has reached his limit and flies into a violent rage, attempting to kill his wife. The Empress throws herself between them, desperate to save them from each other, heartsick over the conflict she has created. She does not want a shadow stained with blood. The Dyer's Wife, who has never seen this kind of passion flare from her husband, softens her heart. She tells him that she lied, that she only wanted to see if he cared. She did not commit adultery or sell her shadow. Just as the couple goes to embrace, the Realm of the Spirits and the Realm of the Humans collides. The Dyer's house explodes and is swallowed up by the earth.

In the final scene of the opera, the Dyer and the Dyer's Wife walk aimlessly in the Realm of the Spirits, unable to find each other. They are lost, plagued by love and remorse. The Empress and the Nurse arrive at the entrance of the temple, plagued with their own guilt and terror. They stand at the confluence of the Water of Life and the Threshold of Death. The Nurse fears that the Empress's father, the King, will unleash his wrath upon her for exposing the Empress to the world of humanity. Simultaneously, the Empress feels the imminence of the curse about to turn the Emperor into stone. Her desire for a shadow has now endangered the fate of the human couple and of her husband. She severs her ties with the Nurse and pledges herself to the human race. She has been transformed by the couple's suffering and is willing to forfeit her own life for theirs, meaningful and true. On Earth, she witnessed how even with pain, the freedom to love and live exists. In the Realm of the Spirits, she was imprisoned by the Emperor, who viewed her as his possession. Their extravagant life offered no freedom.

Just as the Nurse is banished to the Underworld by the Red Falcon for her duplicity and deception, the Empress is invited to drink from the fountain of the Water of Life by one of the Spirit Messengers. When she does, she is told that the shadow of the Dyer's Wife will be hers and the Emperor will not turn to stone.

The Spirit Messenger hands her a gold chalice filled with the alchemical waters and urges the Empress to drink deeply. Above the sound of bubbling waters she hears the distress cries of the lost couple searching for each other. In a moment of sharp anguish and clarity, the Empress cries out, "I will not!"

The fountain vanishes, and instantaneously a shadow is cast behind the Empress.

The Red Falcon appears, and the curse is lifted. The Emperor is released from the bondage of stone. He experiences the force of his wife and sees her for the first time as an individual apart from himself. She has passed the trials imposed on her. In following her own heart and proclaiming the power of her own voice, the Empress finds her shadow and frees her husband from bondage.

The Empress's selfless act of resistance, her refusal to drink water tainted with the blood of pain and corruption, has transformed her into an authentic human being. Courage gives birth to her shadow. Through her shadow, she has found her voice. With her voice, she calls forth integrity. The Dyer and the Dyer's Wife are reunited. The voices of their unborn children rejoice. Harmony is restored.

The Empress and Emperor, the Dyer and the Dyer's Wife celebrate the convergence of darkness and light. Peace is proclaimed. Jubilation abounds. Their shadows cast together create the Bridge of Unity.

My father was rapt. We both were. For more than three hours we were carried into this fairy tale. I saw myself in each of the characters: the controller and the controlled; the privileged and the oppressed; the woman without the shadow and the woman who didn't honor the shadow she had. Myths have a way of bringing what is unconscious to the surface and putting a face on what we cannot see.

Something began to resolve itself in me.

Each time the Red Falcon appeared, the fluttering of wings was expressed through the flute. *Peter and the Wolf* prepared me for this journey. As musical phrases reappeared, they became cairns to follow, leading us along the path of the story. The repetition of notes became a comfort, a place where I could stand in this invented world. A motif, discordant at first, eventually turned into a melody.

Strauss's musical gestures were transformed into tonal poems, created and held in the long, sustaining notes of the characters' arias and duets. Words dissipated into pure feeling. My spirit was soaring.

Would you believe me if I told you when I opened my mouth a bird flew out?

My father was equally moved. During one of the intermissions he told me in a rare moment that because of the power of Mother's presence, he rarely spoke. No need. She covered for him. It was not until after her death that he really began to engage socially.

"People tell me I've become much more gregarious since Diane died," he said. "I am more involved with our friends now." He paused. "I've learned a lot from living alone. When I hear that someone has lost a spouse or child, the next day I just knock on their door. It doesn't matter what I say. What matters is I am there."

My father is more involved in our lives, as well. His voice is increasingly tender, a tone we rarely knew as children except through his actions. The same was true of our grandfather Jack. We really did not know him until after Mimi died.

Together, my father and I not only listened to the arc of Strauss's heartbreaking and triumphant music, but we felt the full register of the human condition within ourselves. I wished I had held his hand, but I didn't dare. The operatic voices painted with great intensity and conviction became the colors of passion and pain within Hofmannsthal's ambitious libretto.

As the opera ended, we stood up in the loges of the opera house side by side, applauding wildly as the curtain closed.

My Mother's Journals are an applause of white gloves, an encore each time one is opened.

Myths can make a reality more intelligible.
—Jenny Holzer

My Mother's Journals are a myth.

LIII

M Y MOTHER *left me her journals, and all her journals were blank.*

My mother's journals are a shadow play with mine. I am a woman wedded to words. Words cast a shadow. Without a shadow there is no depth. Without a shadow there is no substance. If we have no shadow, it means we are invisible.

As long as I have a shadow, I am alive.
as long as I have a shadow

The Woman Without a Shadow whose name is the Empress is not a human being, but a prisoner in the Realm of the Spirits held captive by her husband. We are all held captive by something.

My mother's prison was her prescribed role.

My mother played a role.

Many roles.

Mother has a name, Diane Dixon Tempest. I will speak her name. She did not write in her journals, but she did write letters to her family and kept all her talks that she gave in church.

During the push for the Equal Rights Amendment, which she supported, she delivered these words to her community of women within the Relief Society:

It is important for women to be educated. I think it takes more know-how and courage to be a proper woman these days as never before. There is no excuse for an LDS woman not to know and understand the issues involved in the ERA . . . One of the good things to come out of Women's Rights Movements around the world over the years is the intellectual awakening that has come to women themselves. The degree of our aliveness depends on the degree of our awareness . . .

In the just living of life, in the rush of days, it is so easy to get our priorities mixed. How do we find time through our busy schedule of being a mother and a wife to find self development for ourselves . . .

Do you ever wonder sometimes if your family thinks of you as a series of functions rather than a person . . . I go through phases where I stop and ask myself who really am I? Do I have my own identity besides being someone's wife and someone's mother? What should I become? What should I be doing now at this time of my life? . . .

"There are two important days in a woman's life: the day she is born and the day she finds out why."

She then recounted the story of Mary and Martha:

Mary and Martha were good friends of Jesus. After Jesus entered their home, Mary sat at His feet and listened to His words, but Martha busied herself with preparations for their guest.

Martha, troubled about many things, had let her priorities become mixed. Preparation for the house had come before the more important priority: the visit of the guest himself.

I folded my mother's talk and placed it in one of her journals she refused to write in. Through the years, she kept buying one after another, but just couldn't write a word in them and remain true to herself. My mother's journals are her shadow. They hold her depth and substance and her refusal to be known.

My mother refused her roles.

"I will not," cried the Empress in the full power of her voice. She refused to drink from the golden fountain bubbling with the Water of Life, because it would have been at someone else's expense. If my mother had written the truth of her life, she both believed and feared it would be at someone else's expense. She did not want to hurt those she loved if her journals were read. And we are raised to believe our journals will be read by the future.

The future was a luxury Mother never had. She lived in the white-hot flame of each day. At thirty-eight, she faced her own mortality and lived until Hank, her last-born son, turned twenty. She finished raising her children, a vow she had made to herself.

The will of women is the will of Life.

The last lines of Strauss's opera *Die Frau ohne Schatten* are sung by the unborn children: "Mother . . . the trouble that perplexed you . . . Would there ever be a feast if we were not, secretly, at once the guests and also the hosts!"

The nature of living and loving is the act of reciprocity. As women, we are told that to be the guest is to receive. We are told that to be the host is to give. But what if it is the reverse? What if it is the guest who gives to the host and it is the host who receives from the guest each time she sets her table to welcome and feed those she loves? To be the guest and the host simultaneously is to imagine a mutual exchange of gifts predicated on respect and joy. If we could adopt this truth, perhaps we as women would be less likely to become martyrs.

Setting the table.

What are we setting the table for?

Mother and Mimi are in conversation.

Mimi speaks: "Transformation, Diane."

LIV

M**Y VOICE** rises again and again in beauty within the wonder and awe of the spectacle: an exaltation of larks; the murmuration of starlings; a murder of crows; a parliament of owls. And then in the privacy of truth, there is still the repeating courage of one hermit thrush, hidden in the woods, singing between intervals of thunder. It is not in sorrow that I am moved to speak or act, but in the beauty of what remains. An albatross on Midway Atoll, dead and decomposing, is now a nest of feathers harboring plastic from the Pacific gyre of garbage swirling in the sea. We can kneel in horror and beg forgiveness. Or we can turn away. But the albatross crying overhead, buoyed up by the breeze, is suspended in air by her vast bridge of wings. She is the one who beckons us to respond.

"I am not a criminal! I didn't kill anybody!" the boy cried. "I just wanted to kill myself."

We watched the fifteen-year-old boy writhing in pain after he attempted to slit his wrists. He was accompanied by a policeman who by law had to place him in handcuffs.

I was sitting inside the waiting room of the Maine Medical Coast Clinic with, mostly, injured lobstermen.

I had apologized to the clerk after entering the emergency room. "For what?" she asked. For overreacting. Now, after my symptoms had been described, blood pressure noted, and temperature taken, I was waiting to see if that was true.

It was past midnight. After several hours of tests, including a CT scan and an EKG, a physician's assistant ushered me into a private room.

"There is a soft-tissue density on the left side of your brain measuring eleven point eight by eight point six millimeters in maximal dimensions."

I asked her to speak to me in a language I could understand.

"I don't know exactly how to say this," she said, "but it appears you have a brain tumor and you're in the middle of a stroke."

I started to laugh, unable to take in what I had just heard. By then the doctor had walked into the room. Overhearing the conversation and the edges of my humor, she interrupted. "How about this: on a scale of one to ten, you are at an eight."

That got my attention.

I called Brooke in Utah and told him what was happening—the right side of my body was numb, my vision was blurred and my speech slurred. He listened and said little. He said he would be on the next plane as soon as he could get to the airport. Castle Valley was flooding. Friends and neighbors were sandbagging Placer Creek in the middle of the night, hoping to save homes in its path. Ours was one of them. He took the phone outside, where I could hear what sounded like thunder as the rising river roared through the arroyo past our house.

I saw the falcon that slit my eye. It was following its prey, darting through canyons above a turbulent river with the velocity of a bullet. This time it hit me. Blind. Blindsided. I am inside an eddy, unable to escape the violence of a whirlpool, caught in the circling terror of my own thoughts.

Like a flash flood in the desert, it doesn't have to be raining before the water hits. I always believed my mortality would arrive on wings of grace, not through a numbing of my body that would prevent me from walking or finding my way toward words.

I kept thinking, *This is not my story, this is not my story*, until out of utter exhaustion I surrendered to the comfort of fatigue and the reality of the cold, hard gurney I was lying on, covered by a thin cotton blanket. *So this is where I am*, I thought. *How surprising.*

As if the falcon had settled on a ledge, my mind calmed, able to grasp a different vantage point. *What if I do have a brain tumor? How shall I live? What if I am in the middle of a stroke? How shall I live? What if I am fine and this is all a mistake?* And then I realized, in the darkness of my inquiry, the outcome didn't matter, the question remained the same.

The nurse came in to take my temperature. She flipped on the lights. I sat up, squinted, and looked at the clock. The two black hands on the white face began to rotate wildly. Twenty-four hours circled in seconds.

"No, it's not your brain," said the nurse matter-of-factly, seeing my confusion. "The hands are circling the clock. And I can't tell you why this is happening."

Back in Salt Lake City, I am given a definitive diagnosis: I have a cavernous hemangioma located in what doctors call the "eloquent" part of my brain, or Wernicke's brain, the home of language comprehension, where metaphor and the patterned mind live. It is a small tangle of vessels, likely benign, resembling a raspberry, with pockets of pooled blood bunched together. In simple terms, I had a bleed and therefore went numb. It could happen again anytime. Prior bleeds predict future bleeds. Treatment comes in two forms: brain surgery or wait and watch.

The conversation with the neurosurgeon went like this: "I will cut a ring of bone from your skull. We will enter the brain and, while you are conscious, run some tests of comprehension to see where the no-fly zones are, the areas we need to avoid to make sure there is as little risk to your language center as possible. After that, we'll put you under, remove the malformation, put the circle of bone back in place, cover it with a six-inch plate of titanium with screws, put back your skin flap, stitch it closed, and wait and see how you recover."

"Meaning?" I asked.

"Meaning, we'll have to wait and see if you can understand what I say or can speak."

I stopped listening.

I asked him if I could see the image of my brain one more time. With a click on the computer, my cavernoma appeared back on the X-ray screen. I stared at the black-and-white image. It was unclear whether I was looking at a bullet hole or a window of light.

Doctors delivering second and third opinions from the University of Utah to the Columbia University Department of Neurology all asked the same question: "How well do you live with uncertainty?"

"What else is there?" I said.

I opt to do nothing.

For weeks, months after my diagnosis, I dreamed of birds.

*My Mother's Journals when opened by the wind
become the wings of birds, white birds.*

White birds. White peacocks. White owls. White doves and crows. These white birds in my dreams inhabit a frozen landscape accompanied by white bears and wolves, and I wonder what is frozen in me, what has rendered me numb in a world I thought I was so open to feeling.

The body doesn't lie.

In the deepest winter of 2010, I was in Maine attending the memorial service of a beautiful young woman. Gifted with words, she was a promising writer who had just graduated from college. From time to time, we exchanged essays and stories. She was smart, irreverent, and undone by the pull of her own perfection. To say that she lost herself to anorexia is to imply that we don't share her geography of panic. We do. *I will never be enough. I want to disappear.* The collective struggle became personal. She was tired. She was resolved. She took her life. And as a community gathered around her beloved parents and brother, we all bore the burden of responsibility and regrets.

Inside the church, all the ushers were fathers, and it was the mothers who brought offerings of food throughout the week to the bereaved house, serving the family as they became guests in their own home, comforted. And I thought about how we parent each other through grief in gestures large and small. My eyes focused on the elegantly crafted box—made by the hands of a neighbor—now holding her ashes, *ashes, we all fall down*. The woods she ran through as a child hold her in memories of maple, birch, and balsam fir. Pink tulips soften the edges of the altar. Emily's favorite flower. Yes, I will speak her name, her beautiful name, *Emily*.

Do any of us ever fully understand the consequences of our actions?

Winter's searing light burned through the stained-glass windows of the white-steepled church as we listened to the pastor read from "The Judgment of the Birds" by Loren Eiseley:

> The sun was warm there, and the murmurs of forest life blurred softly away into my sleep. When I awoke, dimly aware of some commotion and outcry in the clearing, the light was slanting down through the pines in such a way that the glade was lit like some vast cathedral. I could see the dust motes of wood pollen in the long shaft of light, and there on the extended branch sat an enormous raven with a red and squirming nestling in his beak.
>
> The sound that awoke me was the outraged cries of the nestling's parents, who flew helplessly

in circles about the clearing. The sleek black monster was indifferent to them. He gulped, whetted his beak on the dead branch a moment and sat still. Up to that point the little tragedy had followed the usual pattern. But suddenly, out of all that area of woodland, a soft sound of complaint began to rise. Into the glade fluttered small birds of half a dozen varieties drawn by the anguished outcries of the tiny parents.

No one dared to attack the raven. But they cried there in some instinctive common misery, the bereaved and the unbereaved. The glade filled with their soft rustling and their cries. They fluttered as though to point their wings at the murderer. There was a dim intangible ethic he had violated, that they knew. He was a bird of death.

And he, the murderer, the black bird at the heart of life, sat on there, glistening in the common light, formidable, unmoving, unperturbed, untouchable.

The sighing died. It was then I saw the judgment. It was the judgment of life against death. I will never see it again so forcefully presented. I will never hear it again in notes so tragically prolonged. For in the midst of protest, they forgot the violence. There, in that clearing, the crystal note of a song sparrow lifted hesitantly in the hush. And finally, after painful fluttering, another took the song, and then another, the song passing from one bird to another, doubtfully at first, as though some evil thing were being slowly forgotten. Till suddenly they took heart and sang from many throats joyously together as birds are known to sing. They sang because life is sweet and sunlight beautiful. They sang under the brooding shadow of the raven. In simple truth they had forgotten the raven, for they were the singers of life, and not of death.

I walked out of the church into the bitter cold. A painted bunting, normally not seen north of the Carolinas, had flown in on the tail of a blizzard, been blown off course, and stayed. I, too, had been blown off course. I needed to see that bird. I made a house call to the man whose feeder it was frequenting. Turns out he was the pastor to all the islands in Penobscot Bay.

"Come back at six forty-five tomorrow morning," he said. "He's been pretty punctual."

And so I kept my date with the painted bunting, driving in the dark down a snow-packed road in coastal Maine. I knocked on the door. The pastor opened it and invited me inside. His wife had three cups of coffee brewing. The only light in their home emanated from the woodstove in the kitchen, where a large picture window framed the feeder outside. It was 6:30 a.m. We sat with long pauses between words. Mainers are never ones to say too much. At 6:43 a.m. the painted bunting arrived, like a dream between the crease of shadow and light. His silhouette grew toward color for the seven short minutes he stayed. And when dawn struck his tiny feathered back, he ignited like a flame: red, blue, and green. There were no other birds around him. He was alone with his singular tapping on the lip of the feeder, eating one sunflower seed at a time, and then he flew—

I have not dreamed of white birds since.

My Mother's Journals are closed.

A month later, another accidental appointment. I step into the Spheris Gallery in Hanover, New Hampshire. I find myself standing in front of a spiral of birds—black, black-gray, gray-white, red—in the cutout shapes of swallows and swifts. These birds gain momentum against a white wall. Each bird flutters and flies according to the length of the pin that keeps it in place.

Black-white; black; black-gray; red; red-gray; blue—these birds create an unexpected velocity even in the gallery. *Red Swirl* is an installation created by Julia Barello, an artist who lives in New Mexico. She understands swifts and swallows, how they toy with tawdry heat waves playing off redrock walls.

The gallery is empty. I pull up a chair. The spiral of birds registers as a joyous familiarity, alive in the desert, alive in me. And yet something is not quite right. I feel a disturbance, a quiet wounding. I am holding a question like a trapped bird that is fluttering inside my cupped hands for release.

Each bird bears the burden of text on its wings. Small white sentences, fragments too small to read from afar. I did not notice this peculiarity until now. I stand up and walk toward them for a closer examination. My hair stands on end. These birds are made from the X-ray films of MRIs, magnetic resonant images like the one that exposed the cavernoma in my brain six months earlier.

I pinch the skin on my right hand to see if I am numb.

Each bird is an image is a presence is a person, and I wonder if the people represented here are alive or dead. The partial scans of their brains, their bones, their organs, with letters of their identity here or there, are now re-visioned and reconstructed, but the evidence of a person in peril remains. Like me, an image becomes the diagnosis, determined and named. What cannot be named is a disturbance.

My Mother's Journals are a disturbance.

To be numb to the world is another form of suicide.

I feel myself separating from the sentence written on my own wings. How do we move beyond our own diagnosis? I turn to the birds, the ember of the painted bunting burning in my hands. Of course. Off course. The bunting got caught in a storm and stayed. I have been seized in a storm of my own making. Whirlwind. World-wind. Distracted and displaced. In the wounding of becoming lost, I can correct myself. We can take flight from our lives in a form other than denial and return to our authentic selves through the art of retreat. Accidental sightings, whether witnessed in a brain or on a winter dawn, remind us there is no such thing as certainty. Tulips dance even after their lives have been cut short.

And so we embrace the surprise.

My Mother's Journals are a surprise.

The red bird at the center of this spiral accumulates its own velocity. Say it again: velocity. Words have a velocity. I am a woman of words. Take away my words and what is left of me? The gift of my patterned mind begins to flatten and take flight, leaving me—leaving those close—with no memories of how to apprehend a word like *bird*.

I bleed. I become numb. This frightens me.

My Mother's Journals frighten me.

Now, in a shift of light, the shadows of birds are more pronounced on the gallery's white wall. The shadow of each bird is speaking to me. Each shadow doubles the velocity, ferocity of forms. The shadow, my shadow now merges with theirs. Descension. Ascension. The velocity of wings creates the whisper to awaken.

My Mother's Journals are an awakening.

How shall I live?

I want to feel both the beauty and the pain of the age we are living in. I want to survive my life without becoming numb. I want to speak and comprehend words of wounding without having these words become the landscape where I dwell. I want to possess a light touch that can elevate darkness to the realm of stars.

This vascular malformation could bleed and burst. Or I can simply go on living, appreciating my condition as a vulnerable human being in a vulnerable world, guided by the songs of birds. What is time, sacred time, but the acceleration of consciousness? There are so many ways to change the sentences we have been given.

———

We cannot do it alone. We do it alone.

> The human mind always makes progress but it is
> a progress in spirals.
>
> —Madame de Staël

How shall we live?

Once upon a time, when women were birds, there was the simple understanding that to sing at dawn and to sing at dusk was to heal the world through joy. The birds still remember what we have forgotten, that the world is meant to be celebrated.

My Mother's Journals are to be celebrated.

LIV(E)

I HEAR MY MOTHER'S VOICE—not outwardly, but inwardly—while walking the Spiral Jetty on the edge of Great Salt Lake. The water has receded, and a spiral of stones curl inside themselves, creating a path toward the center.

Louis and I walk the spiral in silence. We are with two friends, a man and woman, who also walk the spiral in silence. I have never seen Robert Smithson's sculpture until now. I have been waiting for a time when I would be in need of ceremony.

The salt crystals are shimmering prisms of light as the heat emanating from the dry lake bed creates a distortion of time and space. We are floating in a dreamscape of desert and water and sky. My inland sea, my basin of tears now evaporated, holds us and sustains me. It has been twenty-four years since Mother's death, and never has she felt more present. In this layered landscape I see the surrounding changes, but more important, I feel them. Once covered by the rising Great Salt Lake, the Spiral Jetty is now exposed. Like me—my own heart is uncovered. Great Salt Lake glistens on the horizon like a silver blade.

I thought I was writing a book about voice. I thought I would proclaim as a woman that we must speak the truth of our lives at all costs. But what I realize with Louis walking behind me is that I will never be able to say what is in my heart, because words fail us, because it is in our nature to protect, because there are times when what is public and what is private must be discerned. There is comfort in keeping what is sacred inside us not as a secret, but as a prayer.

The world is already split open, and it is in our destiny to heal it, each in our own way, each in our own time, with the gifts that are ours.

We stand in the center of the spiral and turn in the vast quiet that presses in on us. It is disorienting. The men leave. The women stay, and together we lie down on the salt desert, facing each other, our ears on the Earth, listening.

I hear my mother's voice.

In the emptiness of this beloved landscape that has embraced me all my life, I hold my mother's journals as another paradox, journals without words that create a narrative of the imagination.

My mother's gift is the Mystery.

Each day I begin with the empty page.